The *Fenway* HOTEL

The GRAND LADY of DUNEDIN

Her Struggles, Successes, and Survival

SECOND EDITION

Praises for

The Fenway Hotel

The Grand Lady of Dunedin
– Her Struggles, Successes, and Survival

"This book is a must read for anybody interested in the history of Dunedin and to learn the full story of one of Dunedin's iconic historic structures."

– Vinnie Luisi, Director, Dunedin Historical Museum

"Beautifully and diligently researched; full of fascinating little known facts about the Fenway Hotel over the years and its metamorphosis into Trinity Bible College and Schiller International University.
Now, after years of neglect, the Fenway Hotel will be transformed once again.
Special thanks to Trudy Kelly for her fantastic Fenway history journey!"

– Bill Sweetnam, Dunedin resident

"The book looks great and the facts about SIU are correct- brings back wonderful memories.
Schiller was a special place, bringing people together from all over the world, kind of like a mini UN. Thanks for keeping Dunedin's heritage alive."

– Markus Leibrecht, Former Director of International Admissions, Schiller International University

"The book is well researched, well written and fun to look back in time. I wish I could go back and mingle with the people and enjoy all the amenities of a grand hotel."

– Kathleen Kelly Giddings, Retired Business Manager, Atlanta, GA

"Trudy Kelly brings the Fenway Hotel in Dunedin to life. I would fully recommend this book to any person who has a love of interesting histories, because the Fenway Hotel has certainly had one."

– Maranda Vilsack, Student and Peer Tutor, St. Petersburg College

The Fenway HOTEL

The GRAND LADY of DUNEDIN

Her Struggles, Successes, and Survival

SECOND EDITION

WILLIAM N. KELLY
Consulting & Publishing, Inc.

by Trudy Kelly

The Fenway Hotel:
The Grand Lady of Dunedin – Her Struggles, Successes, and Survival, 2nd Edition
Copyright ©2018 by William N. Kelly

International Standard Book Number:
978-0-9886513-5-7

Printed in the United States of America

Library of Congress Catalog-In-Publication Data
Kelly, TA
The Fenway Hotel: The Grand Lady of Dunedin – 2nd Ed © 2018
Includes bibliographic references
Control Number: 2015910423

William N. Kelly Consulting & Publishing, Inc.
www.williamnkelly.com
3060 Braeloch Circle, East Clearwater, FL 33761

Cover designed by Eli Blyden ~ The Book Guy,
CrunchTime Graphics

Cover photograph of the Fenway Hotel ©2014 Frank Duffy

975.963 Kelly

Dedication

This book is dedicated to the early Dunedin residents who financed and built the Fenway Hotel and to others after them who saw the beauty of this hotel and continued its legacy.

It is also dedicated to Trinity College and Schiller International University whose students gave life and purpose to the hotel.

Special recognition to George Rahdert, whose dream of restoring the Fenway to its former glory unfortunately didn't happen, and to the Taoist Tai Chi Society and Mainsail Lodging & Development who are giving the hotel new life.

Table of Contents

Foreword

One of Dunedin's pride and joys in the 1930's and 1940's was the new luxurious hotel facing St. Joseph Sound known as the Fenway Hotel.

The Fenway Hotel is interesting for so many reasons. Many individuals are fascinated by its architectural style, the individuals and celebrities who stayed there, and its historical involvement with the community of Dunedin.

For many years the history of the Fenway has been stored in various institutions and has never been compiled as one full historical and factual resource. This is where Trudy Kelly's story begins. In the 1990's Schiller University used the Fenway as its home. Trudy was Schiller's librarian and fell in love with the building and its story.

When Schiller University moved its location to Largo, the Fenway closed down, but was not forgotten. Trudy started a personal collection of Fenway material that included artifacts from the building, postcards, and many copies of the Dunedin Times that highlighted the Fenway's activities.

With the many sources to peruse through, Trudy started to gather the complete story beginning with its construction in the 1920's to its recent acquisition by the Taoist Tai Chi Society whose plan is to totally revitalize the Fenway's beauty. What you have before you is Trudy's hours of reading microfilm, books, newspapers, and old scrapbooks full of Fenway memories.

Trudy's book about the Fenway is a detailed story that includes the important individuals involved with this historic building, details of its classic Spanish-Mediterranean style architecture and the interesting highs and lows of the Fenway's history.

– Vinnie Luisi
Director, Dunedin Historical Museum

Preface

My appreciation of the Fenway Hotel began in 2005 when I worked as a librarian at Schiller International University. At the time, the University was located at the Fenway Hotel in Dunedin.

The more I became acquainted with the hotel, the more I wanted to learn its history. I started collecting articles, photographs, and postcards of the hotel in order to tell its story.

The story of the Fenway Hotel is one of survival. The hotel was vacant three times and managed to survive the Great Depression (1929-1940); World War II (1939-1945); the economic decline in 2007, and other hard economic times.

To discover the history of the Fenway it was necessary to research in many places – newspaper articles, websites, published and unpublished histories, brochures, advertisements, and postcards.

My goal was to take this information and offer a comprehensive story of the Fenway Hotel. As a researcher, I had to sort facts from fiction, and try to document the truth to the best of my ability.

People ask me why the hotel was named the Fenway and is there any connection with Fenway Park in Boston. As far as I know, there is no connection with the stadium, but there is a similarity.

Fenway Park was named for a neighborhood in Boston called the Fenway neighborhood. The Fenway Hotel is located in an area in Dunedin called Fenway-on-the-Bay.

These two areas were probably named after "fen," which is low land covered wholly or partially with water, a boggy land.

People advised me to include a "ghost story" or two in this book. There were Schiller students who talked about experiencing ghosts in the Fenway, but I cannot corroborate these stories and the students are long gone. I will just have to leave it up to the readers to decide if there were spirits living in the hotel or the students just imagined them.

Why the need for a second edition? So much has happened since the publication of the first edition of this book, so I wanted to make sure "the rest of the story" was documented.

I hope readers find this history to be as fascinating as I do. If they do, I have succeeded in telling the story of the Fenway.

- Trudy Kelly, MLS

Acknowledgements

I would like to thank the Dunedin Historical Museum for their help in supplying so much of the hotel's history found in Dunedin newspapers and scrapbooks located in the museum. Without their resources I wouldn't have had much of a story. Their appreciation of the Fenway Hotel helped me recognize there was a need for documenting its history.

Special thanks also to photographer, Frank Duffy, for use of his beautiful photographs of the Fenway.

I would like to thank and acknowledge the loving assistance from my husband, Dr. William Kelly, who supported my writing of this book. His experience writing and publishing books helped me tremendously. He read and reread my drafts, and gave me useful suggestions and encouragement.

The Fenway HOTEL

The GRAND LADY of DUNEDIN

Her Struggles, Successes, and Survival

SECOND EDITION

THE FENWAY HOTEL

Chapter 1

A New Hotel in Dunedin

1924-1926

News that a new hotel might be built in Dunedin was first reported in the *Dunedin Times* on July 3, 1924. A drawing of the proposed hotel was shown. The reason given for building the hotel was the rapid growth of Dunedin required more hotel accommodations.

To build the hotel, the Fenway Hotel Company was incorporated and capital stock of $300,000 at $100 per share was sold. The proposed hotel was described as a large tourist hotel, built in an area known as Fenway-on-the Bay, which was a short distance from the Dunedin downtown.[1]

Residents of Dunedin were encouraged to help fund this project. The *Dunedin Times* (July 10, 1924) said the project needed the backing of the entire community. Enough people had given financially to justify continuing the hotel project, but support was still needed. Residents were asked to "do your part, dig down in your jeans and dish out the necessary coin."[2]

In September, 1924, builders started on the Fenway. Watching the hotel become a reality was exciting for the promoters of the project and for the citizens who thought it would never happen.[3]

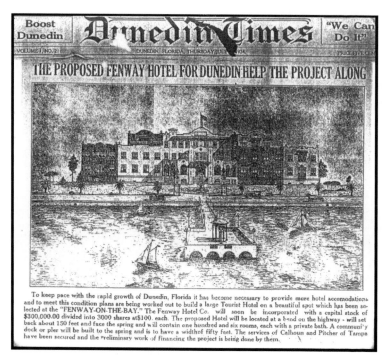

Dunedin Times, July 3, 1924

Description of the Fenway

The Fenway was described as a three-story Mediterranean Revival Style hotel overlooking St. Joseph Sound and Clearwater Bay. The hotel was constructed of "brick and hollow tile with an exterior of stucco with soft terra cotta trimming and decorative tile".[4] There was a circular drive with large, wide steps leading to the front porch.

Some of the descriptions of the Fenway in the early years were "luxury resort hotel;" "finest exclusive resort;" "large tourist hotel on Fenway-on-the-Bay;" and "one of the West Coast's finest resort clubs."

Fenway Under Construction

Architect of the Fenway

Herman Everett Wendell was the architect of the Fenway Hotel. His obituary, published in *The Evening Independent* on February 25, 1937, told that he had lived in St. Petersburg for twenty-seven years and was an architect and an inventor.

He designed and supervised construction of both the Fenway Hotel in Dunedin and the Suwannee Hotel in St. Petersburg (also built in 1924). He also invented several types of citrus crates during his lifetime.[5]

George H. Bowles Bought Majority of Stock

Not enough stock was sold to the public to finish the construction of the Fenway. In the July 31, 1925 edition of the *Clearwater Sun*, an article reported a deal was completed the night before that changed ownership of the

Fenway Hotel. At the time, it was still unfinished and financially troubled.

George H. Bowles, a real estate entrepreneur and developer, purchased the rest of the stock for $250,000. The original stockholders requested that they be included. Other stockholders who retained stock in the newly organized corporation were: Dr. A.B. McQueen, E.A. White, H.E. Wendell (architect of the hotel), A.J. Durant (president of the city council of St. Petersburg) and W.H. Armston.[6]

Bowles planned to go to Winter Haven to find a manager to run the hotel when it opened for the season, then go to New York, Boston and Portland, Maine, to find people to finance the Fenway project.[6]

A Radio Station Came to Dunedin

The first commercial radio station in Pinellas County began at the Fenway Hotel. At the time, commercial broadcasting was less than five years old. George Bowles was an early radio enthusiast and had an interest in radio broadcasting.

Before the Fenway was finished, Bowles purchased a used transmitter from the Atlanta Journal's radio station, WSB, to be installed at the hotel. W. Walter Tison, brought the equipment to Dunedin from Atlanta, installed it, and stayed on as "Director of Broadcasting." Bowles' initials - (WGHB) - were used as the radio station's call letters.[7]

The Equipment Arrived

On August 13, 1925 the equipment from Atlanta arrived and was installed on the roof of the hotel. The new station had a capacity of 500 watts, but as soon as the government agreed, the wattage would be boosted to 750 watts.[7]

The studio was located on the third floor of the hotel with a transmitter and a temporary antenna rigged on the roof so the station could begin transmitting programs. A long ladder was used to climb up to the studio.[8]

Work began to build a ground-level studio in the hotel. The walls of the studio were plastered and treated with one-inch thick hair felt on the walls to make the room echo proof. This cost approximately $1500. Equipment was purchased so events held downtown could be broadcast. Regular church services were transmitted over telephone wires to the Fenway.[9]

Dedication of the Station

A 6-hour dedication program was held on December 10, 1925. The studio was moved to the ground floor in time for the dedication. This made it more accessible to those attending the program. People interested in broadcasting were invited to the station that night.

Those wanting to go inside the studio did so before the program started and a member of the staff explained the many features of the studio. Since visitors could not go into the studio during the broadcast, a large plate glass window was installed so the performances could be seen.[10]

The Dedication Program was opened by George H. Bowles. After he gave a dedication address, he introduced Walter Tison, Director of Broadcasting, who outlined the policies and future plans for the station. Mr. Tison was the announcer during the program that followed.[10]

After the formal opening of the station, four hundred fifty-two (452) telegrams from 26 states and Canada poured in from people saying they had heard the dedication program. One of the telegrams was as far away as St. Paul, Alaska, approximately 8,000 miles from Dunedin.[8]

The reason the station could be heard from so far away was the number of radio stations was small, so interference between stations was minimal. In the early days of radio, people "twirled the dials" to find stations. They came upon WGHB and learned about Florida, Dunedin, and the Fenway.[8]

Early Programming

Vera Williamson, manager of the Dunedin Chamber of Commerce, presented a weekly program that reported Chamber activities. She told of the challenge of climbing the long ladder to get to the studio. She managed to make it up and down the ladder every week without slipping.[8]

At the time, there were no "news tickers" to relay news to radio stations, so Tison read articles from *Time Magazine*.[8] Grace Clark was the host of a children's program and was known as the "Story Lady."[11]

In April 26, 1926 W. Walter Tison announced WGHB would air organ recitals from Peace Memorial Presbyterian Church. A special wire connected the studio at the Fenway Hotel to the church in Clearwater.[12]

On January 10, 1927, WGHB sent out their first daytime radio program to the north. Radio engineers in northern cities felt the reception of the program was perfect, even though they feared that static during the day would be a problem. Because of this success, daytime programs aired each afternoon throughout the winter.[13]

Finishing the Fenway

October, 1926 the hotel was still not finished. *The Evening Independent* told that interests in the hotel, owned by George H. Bowles, were purchased.

The other stockholders and holders of liens on the property, along with civic organizations of Dunedin, formed a corporation. They had to untangle the complicated affairs of the Fenway. They got together through civic organizations so Dunedin could finish the hotel and provide accommodations for winter visitors that season.[14]

J. L. Kelly, of the law firm of Kelly, Rives, and Casler stated – "Original stockholders and those holding liens against the project have agreed to take stock in the new company to the amount of their claims."[14]

Judge Freeman Lane of the circuit court signed an order permitting resumption of construction work on the building. It was financed by issuing $150,000 worth of receiver's certificates.[14]

George Smoyer, receiver of the hotel company, announced – "Interests in the corporation had been purchased and a closed corporation was formed so the hotel could be completed."[15]

It was hoped that the hotel would be open for winter visitors.

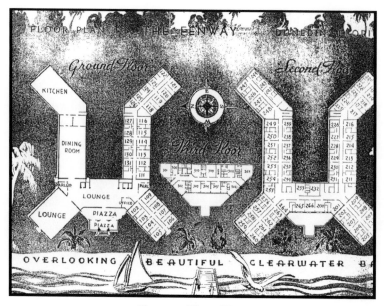

Fenway Floor Plan

Bowles Sold the Radio Station

The radio station became too expensive for Bowles to keep. In the spring of 1926, Edward A. Haley, builder and owner of the Fort Harrison Hotel in Clearwater purchased WGHB.[16]

The aerial towers moved to the city park on South Osceola Avenue in Clearwater and the radio studio moved to the Clearwater Community House, 118 S. Osceola Avenue in Clearwater on November 3, 1926. The call letters of the station changed to WFHH (Ford Harrison Hotel).[17]

In June, the Clearwater Chamber of Commerce acquired the station and the next month the St. Petersburg Chamber of Commerce bought half interest in the station. The call letters were changed to WSUN (Why Stay Up North).[18]

Completion of the Fenway

On October 14, 1926, the *Dunedin Times* reported that contracts for finishing and furnishing the hotel were made. Money to complete the hotel was deposited in the Bank of Dunedin.[19]

Fenway Ready to Open

The hotel was ready to open December 15, 1926, but who would run the hotel now that it was finished?

View from the Hotel Front Porch

THE FENWAY HOTEL

Chapter 2

James H. Batchelder Leases the Hotel

1926-1929

In an article in the December 23, 1926, *Dunedin Times*, H. L Baker, director of the Fenway Hotel's completion, reported that a "nationally known hotel operator" would lease the hotel for three years.[1] A week later it was announced the Fenway would be leased by James H. Batchelder, a hotel and resort owner of the Hotel Alpine in North Woodstock, New Hampshire.[2]

Guests made reservations for the 1927 season and plans were made for entertaining them. The Dunedin Isles Golf and Country Club, gulf beaches, facilities for social gatherings, and other nearby enjoyments were available.

An article in the *Dunedin Times* said the Fenway was one of the "most substantially constructed hotels in Florida. The Fenway is so arranged that every room is flooded with sunshine through large windows that displays interesting vistas of sparkling waters, a tree-lined boulevard and landscapes rich with tropical foliage".[1]

Opening Dinner Dance

There was an opening dinner dance held on Saturday evening, January 8, 1927. It cost $2.50 per plate and reservations were required. The dinner-dance was informal, and dinner was served banquet style. There were over 200 reservations and people from Dunedin, Clearwater, St. Petersburg, and Tarpon Springs attended the event.[3]

Source: Advertising Brochure

The Courts Sold the Fenway Hotel

The hotel was open for the 1927-1928 season, but a headline on August 9, 1928, edition of *The Evening Independent* reported – "Fenway Hotel at Dunedin is Sold."[4]

The hotel was bought at a mortgage foreclosure sale by the Title and Trust Company of Florida, a Jacksonville corporation. The bid started at $64,000. This amount was supposed to satisfy a first mortgage issued under a deed held by the trust company, but the $64,000 received at the sale was not considered enough to pay off the mortgage and attorney fees.[4]

On October 1, 1928 an auction took place because the Title and Trust Company of Jacksonville failed to comply with the terms of the purchase and the court ordered the hotel to be advertised again.[5]

Meanwhile, the receiver for the Fenway, George H. Smoyer, failed to make payments on the furnishings, so they were removed in November, 1928 by Albert Pick & Company in Chicago.[6]

The Fenway did not open for the 1929 season.

Batchelder Leased Hotel Dunedin for His Guests

James H. Batchelder had the Fenway pretty much booked for the 1929 season. When he realized that the hotel would not open for the season, he leased the Hotel Dunedin and tried to get the people who were booked at the Fenway to stay at this hotel.[7]

The Fenway was Sold, Twice!

J. Palmer Williams, from Jacksonville, Florida, bought the Fenway from the Circuit Court on March 3, 1929.[8] He bid for it at a receiver's sale, and paid $57,000.[9]

The *St. Petersburg Times* said he was looking forward to getting the hotel ready for the next winter season since it had been closed for the 1928-1929 season. Reservations were already made awaiting the opening of the Fenway.[8]

In July, 1929, James McGill bought the Fenway from J. Palmer Williams for $58,000.[9,10]

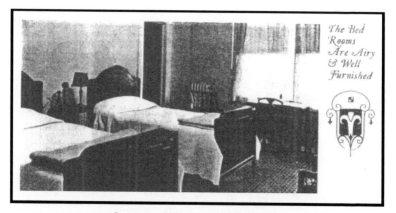

Source: Advertising Brochure

Chapter 3

James McGill Buys the Fenway: It Becomes a Fabulous Hotel

1929-1945

In July, 1929, James McGill bought the Fenway Hotel for $58,000. This began a period when the Fenway ran continuously as one of the finest hotels in the area. When McGill purchased the Fenway, he was running the McGill Manufacturing Company in Valparaiso, Indiana.[1]

McGill was born in 1869 on a farm near Hebron, Indiana. In 1905 he borrowed $5,000 and started his own manufacturing company which became successful.[1]

McGill Came to Florida

In 1910, McGill was sent to Florida for his health. He loved Florida, so in 1919 he purchased a home in St. Petersburg. In 1928, he was driving to the PGA golf course in Dunedin and saw a "For Sale" sign on the front yard of the Fenway Hotel. He felt that buying this hotel would be a good investment.[1]

An article in the *Dunedin Times* on July 18, 1929 was titled – "Fenway Hotel Purchased by Indiana Man." The article said "This transaction brings to an end the legal difficulties which have handicapped operation of the hotel since its completion about four years ago."[2]

C.T. Scanlon Managed the Hotel

McGill made C.T. Scanlan Manager of the Fenway Hotel. Scanlan was McGill's son-in-law and previously had managed the Madrid Hotel in St. Petersburg. He directed the work of furnishing, redecorating, and making improvements to the Fenway.[2]

Scanlan was quoted as saying – "We believe that the Hotel Fenway is the most attractive property of its kind we have ever seen. It is situated on the shores of a beautiful body of water not surpassed by any place in the world. It is near the best golf course in Florida and has close at hand the opportunities for every kind of recreation, fishing, and sailing."[3]

Ready for the Winter Season

By August of 1929, people driving by the Fenway noticed that the appearance of the hotel had changed for the better. A large amount of work was completed on the grounds and the workmen had the hotel ready for the tourist season. The Fenway, after being closed for almost two years, was renovated from top to bottom.[4]

Fenway Opened for the 1929-1930 Season

The Fenway Hotel opened for the 1929-1930 season on December 27, 1929. Some of the guests waited in the area to register at the hotel. Advance bookings for the hotel indicated there would be a large number of registrations for the season. Room rates included breakfast, lunch, and dinner ("American Plan").[5]

Many guests traveled on the Atlantic Coast Line to the Dunedin Railroad Depot. A hotel limousine met them and drove them to the hotel. There was no need for guests to have cars, since most of the entertainment was at or near the hotel.[1]

One of the reasons the hotel was successful was Scanlan offered entertainment for the wives of the golfers. He felt that lack of activities for the wives of avid golfers was a problem for many resort hotels. Scanlan planned programs throughout the day and then planned programs in the evening, so golfers and fishermen could participate along with their wives.

The hotel was strictly high class, completely staffed, beautifully furnished, and offered excellent meals. Scanlan knew that a successful hotel would mean prosperity and growth for Dunedin.[3]

First Season Successful

In January, 1930, Scanlan announced that the hotel was filling up rapidly. Reservations were coming in and it looked like the 116-room hotel would be filled by January 15th.[6] Thus, the first season under the management of C.T. Scanlan was highly successful.

The hotel closed for the season on April 1, 1930. Many guests made reservations for the next season before they left.[7]

Activities at the Fenway

Mr. and Mrs. Scanlan were creative in planning entertainment for their guests. Dinner-dances were held on Saturday evenings, and bridge parties on Monday evenings. Card games such as bridge and another card game, called Konkan, were played on Tuesday evenings.

A 9-hole putting green was installed on the front lawn and lawn golf and putting contests were offered on Thursday afternoons. During the day, golfing parties were able to use the Clearwater Country Club and other area golf courses.

Another activity was a boat chartered for an Anclote River party near Tarpon Springs. There were garden parties, beach parties, dancing, and yachting parties.

Special dinners to celebrate holidays were held every year. The holidays celebrated were: Christmas, New Year's Eve, Lincoln's birthday, Valentine's Day, Washington's birthday, St. Patrick's Day, and sometimes Easter. Colorful menus, flowers, decorations, and entertainment were included to make the dinners special.

Music was a big part of the activities at the Fenway. Recitals, concerts and musical programs were presented every Sunday evening. The Fenway Ensemble played evenings in the lobby of the hotel during the dinner hour and performed the concerts on Sunday evenings. The Ensemble, directed by Harry Van Ham, was made up of a pianist, violinist, and cellist.

At dinner dances music was provided by orchestras, mostly the seven-piece Fenway Orchestra. But there were other orchestras that played for the dinner-dances. Soloists and other performers were part of the entertainment.

Postcard Mailed in 1934

Notable Guests

An article in the February 27, 1938, St. *Petersburg Times*, said, "The Fenway has been a favorite playground for millionaires and notables of the diplomatic, industrial, artistic and literary world."[8]

A noted Chicago lawyer, Clarence Darrow, spent the 1931 winter season at the Fenway. Darrow was a famous criminal lawyer and was the inspiration for the classic novels "Inherit the Wind" (about the Scopes Monkey Trial)" and "To Kill a Mockingbird."[9] He entertained Fenway guests with a special program.[10]

In January, 1933, Senator Robert M. LaFollette, from Wisconsin spent time at the Fenway. LaFollette was a good friend of C.S. McGill, son of the owner, James McGill.[11]

In February, William Felton Barrett (Vice President of the Union Carbon and Carbide Company) and his wife spent time at the hotel.[12]

Fenway Dining Room
Clearwater Sun, May 15, 1983

During the 1934-1935 season Robert Page, a baritone soloist from New York City, stayed at the Fenway while on a concert tour of the south. He was famous for concert work on NBC and starred in the Broadway production of "The Cat and the Fiddler." During his stay, Mr. Page gave a concert in the lounge for guests. [13]

Another guest who stayed during the 1934-1935 season was F.W. Brooks of Chicago, Illinois. He was Sales Manager of the William Wrigley Jr. Company that made chewing gum.[13]

During the 1936-1937 season guests included: Alanson B. Houghton, former ambassador to England and Germany; J.M. Donaldson, noted architect; and Joseph Lincoln, author of stories from Cape Cod and other novels.[14] Dr. James L. McConaughy, President of Wesleyan University, was also a guest that winter.[8]

Captain Robert Bartlett was a visitor to the Fenway in March, 1940. He was an explorer and experienced 42 years exploring the Arctic. He was part of Admiral Peary's expedition and shared his experiences with guests.[15]

Stephen Early, Secretary to President F.D. Roosevelt spent a week at the Fenway in March, 1943. He came for a quiet and much needed rest. Mr. Early was a WWII veteran and had the rank of lieutenant colonel.[16]

Early was associated with Roosevelt since 1913. He was an Associated Press reporter, worked with Roosevelt during the campaign of 1920, was Assistant Secretary to the President in 1933, and then Secretary to the President in July 1, 1937.[16]

While in Dunedin, he rested and played golf. Between games of golf he inspected the Marine base at Dunedin Isles and took rides in an amphibian tractor which was invented by Dunedin resident, Donald Roebling. This amphibian tractor eventually served during WWII as a ship-to-shore transport for men and supplies.[17]

Two distinguished guests who stayed at the hotel in 1943 were K.M. Landis, high commissioner of baseball; and Alfred M. Landon, former Republican presidential candidate.[18]

Improvements to the Fenway

Every year improvements were made to the hotel and grounds to help make guests more comfortable and their experiences more enjoyable.

In November, 1934, a swimming beach was made in front of the hotel. Clean, white sand from gulf beaches was pumped into the bay ninety feet out to complete the beach.[19]

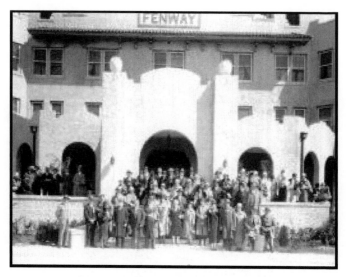

Suncoast News, February 1, 1978
Year photo taken: Late 1920s

During the summer, in 1935, several changes were made. The office was moved, the lobby and dining room were enlarged, and the second floor of the hotel on the north wing, formerly used for servants, was remodeled for use as guest rooms. A 28-car garage was built behind the hotel with a dormitory above it for servants or employees.[20]

When the eighth season (1936-1937) of the Fenway opened, guests enjoyed a new 400-foot pier that was built across from the hotel.[21]

In June, 1938, a channel was dredged from the end of the Fenway dock to the government channel and the dock was extended to 440 feet. The new dock accommodated larger boats that needed seven feet of water to park.[22]

On December 16, 1938 Scanlan built a nine-room Bermuda type cottage facing the Fenway. It was located on

Locklie Street across from the hotel and was leased out for the season. It was known as the "Fenway Cottage"[23]

More Land was Purchased

The rest of the property on the block behind the hotel was purchased during the summer of 1941. The property was cleared and flower gardens planted. An English croquet court and a miniature skeet shooting range were built. Eventually, Scanlan hoped to build a few guest cottages on the property.[24]

Fishing off the Pier
Photo from a scrapbook at the Dunedin Historical Museum

Fenway Guests Became Dunedin Residents

An article in the Dunedin Times reported, "Fenway guests become Dunedin homeowners." It said the hotel was a testing ground for guests who stayed there. Many visitors to this area decided this is where they wanted to live.

Statistics showed that more than 15% of Fenway guests became permanent homeowners or seasonal occupants of homes in the vicinity, and over 65% returned as annual guests of the Fenway.[25]

The Fenway Club

The thirteenth season of the Fenway opened on Saturday, January 3, 1942. Scanlan announced that the Fenway Hotel would change from being a hotel to being a club, known as "The Fenway".[26]

The Effect of WWII

The number of reservations was normal during the war years and Scanlan said there was no indication that WWII affected the number of guests staying at the Fenway.

The Fenway was one of the few hotels open to guests on the Florida West Coast during the war. Most of the hotels in the area were used by the armed forces during WWII.[27]

McGill Sold Fenway to Scanlan

In 1945 McGill sold the Fenway to his son-in-law, C.T. Scanlan.

McGill died on April 26, 1948, three years after he sold the Fenway.

Concert Program, February 4, 1940

THE FENWAY HOTEL

Chapter 4

C.T. Scanlan Buys the Fenway

1945-1956

During the seventeen years that James McGill owned the Fenway, C.T. Scanlan was the manager. The hotel became very successful under Scanlan's leadership, so purchasing the Fenway was a likely development. The price he paid for the hotel was not disclosed.[1]

Before purchasing the hotel in August, Scanlan spent part of the summer of 1945 getting the hotel ready for the new season. He planned a number of improvements that were postponed until after WWII. After the war ended, all rooms were redecorated, the grounds improved, a game room, and modern tennis and shuffleboard courts were added.[2]

Rail transportation was expected to be light, but Scanlan thought gasoline would be available so people could travel to Florida. He believed that the development of a new PGA (Professional Golf Association) golf course in Dunedin would be an important event for Dunedin.

The Fenway catered to a select clientele with guests returning year after year. Many of the guests already named returned, and new names were added to the list of famous guests: Dr. Roscoe C.E. Brown, retired managing editor of the *New York Herald Tribune*; and Senator Harley M. Kilgore from West Virginia.[1]

The Fenway Continued to be Successful

Many guests spent all or part of the season at the Fenway. Activities continued to entertain guests. Dinner dances celebrated the holidays, and bridge and canasta parties were held.

Lobster dinners were offered on Friday evenings at the Scanlan home at 277 Locklie Street, across from the hotel. Lobsters were shipped by air from Maine.[3]

Photo of the Sitting Room

Mrs. Rachel Scanlan Passed Away

C.T. Scanlan's wife, Rachel, passed away on Wednesday, November 5, 1953 after a long illness. She was survived by her husband C.T. Scanlan, daughter Mrs. Kenneth Flowers, and one grandson, Charles. Other survivors were her mother, two brothers, and two sisters.[4]

Scanlan Married Again

After Rachel's death C.T. Scanlan married Doris Scoggins. She helped him run the hotel and entertain guests as Rachel had done previously.[5]

The Fenway was Sold

The August 23, 1956 edition of the *Dunedin Times* reported C.T. Scanlan sold the Fenway to Marius Pauchey.[6]

Scanlan had received other offers to purchase the hotel but waited until he found someone who would run the hotel in the same manner he had. Pauchey was assured that guests, who came year after year, would be willing to return under new management.[6]

Why Did Scanlan Sell the Fenway?

An article, in the *Clearwater Sun*, gave some answers to why he sold the Fenway, despite it being so successful. In 1983, Kathy Sutton interviewed Tommy Scanlan. The interview was held 27 years after he sold the Fenway.[7]

Scanlan told the reporter the first time he saw the 116-room resort hotel, it was half-finished, unfurnished, and in disrepair. He realized it had a certain charm. His father-in-law bought the hotel and they fixed it up.

As manager of the hotel, Scanlan was able to make it a success. Residential hotels depended on guests returning every year, occupying the same suite of rooms. Scanlan said, "They would come here with cars and chauffeurs and three trunks each. They came to hole in."[7]

He said well-known guests stayed at the Fenway, such as defense attorney, Clarence Darrow and poet, Carl Sandburg. He liked Darrow and they would sit for hours playing nickel and dime poker. He remembered Sandburg as sort of a roughneck and was always critical of everything and everybody.

Two other famous guests he talked about were William Cooper Proctor, Proctor & Gamble, and former Kansas Governor Alf Landon, a 1936 Republican Presidential candidate.

Looking back, he wondered why he became involved in the venture. "Those times were some of the roughest times I've seen in Florida when I was trying to start the Fenway. I wonder how I had the courage to get mixed up in that. Times were hard. The war was approaching and Florida's West Coast had not yet been discovered."[7]

The first year was horrible, but three years later the hotel broke even.

"It was Fabulous, it Really Was"

Scanlan said that the Fenway was a first-class establishment that catered to the rich. "That was part of the fun of the Fenway. They were kind of fussy people, but they didn't complain about the price." It cost $20 a day to stay at the hotel. For that price guests had a room with a private bath and three meals a day, cooked by a French chef.

Scanlan had breakfast every morning with the cooks to discuss the day's menu. His first wife, Rachel, and later his second wife, Doris, organized entertainment and arranged flowers for the rooms and lobby. "It was fabulous, it really was," Scanlan said of the hotel.[7]

Daughter Lorrie's Experience

Scanlan's daughter, Lorrie Flowers, grew up in the hotel. She said it was a unique experience. When she thinks of her childhood, "It was a very happy, wonderful experience." She remembers, "feeling spoiled as she dined on fine food in the servants' quarters while her parents dressed up to dine with the guests."[7]

Lorrie said, "My parents were the outgoing, enthusiastic types. They loved people, they loved running the hotel, and they made friends all over the United States and all over the world. It was an exciting place for me to grow up."[7]

After 26 years, Scanlan decided he wanted to do something else. He began to realize that people wanted other types of vacations. "No longer would these people be content sitting in a rocking chair on the piazza and rocking away the season."[7]

Tommy (C.T.) Scanlan after the Fenway

In 1958, Scanlan was named Chairman of the Red Cross Fund Campaign for Dunedin. He served as General Chairman for the Upper Pinellas Chapter of the Red Cross.[8]

In April, 1960, he was Commodore of the Carlouel Yacht Club on Clearwater Beach.[8] In 1962, he was one of the founders of the First Federal Bank of Dunedin and its president until it merged with First Federal of Tampa. He was on its board until 1984 when he retired.[8]

Scanlan Died After an Extended Illness

Charles Townsend "Tommy" Scanlan died on October 18, 1990. He had been ill for several years and needed 24-hour care for a year and a half. He was survived by his wife, daughter, sister, three grandchildren, and five great-grandchildren.[8]

Charles T. Scanlan
Clearwater Sun, May 15, 1983

Cleaning Staff
Photo from a scrapbook at the Dunedin Historical Museum

Bellhops on the steps to the Fenway porch
Photo from a scrapbook at the Dunedin Historical Museum

Chapter 5

Marius Pauchey Opens the Fenway Year-Round

1956-1959

On August 22, 1956, C. Townsend Scanlan sold the Fenway Hotel to Marius J. Pauchey from Clearwater, Florida. Negotiations had been in progress since June of that year.[1] The hotel sold for more than $300,000.[2] Pauchey previously owned other hotels, mostly in the North. He owned the Clearwater Beach Hotel until August 24, 1955, a year before he purchased the Fenway.[3]

There were several projects Pauchey wanted to do. The facilities would continue to operate as a private club, as in the past, but on a larger scale. The Fenway Club was open for membership on a year-round basis for local and winter residents.[1]

Changes for the Fenway

Since there were no swimming pools anywhere in Dunedin, one of the first things Pauchey did was to have one built. A 35' x 70' pool was built in the center of the lawn on the south side of the main building. Construction began October 1, 1956 and the pool was ready for the 1956-1957 season.[2]

1956 Postcard of the Fenway Pool

Both the cocktail lounge and dining room were open to the public. Dunedin residents and winter visitors living elsewhere used the Fenway to entertain friends.[5]

Pauchey managed the hotel, assisted by his son, Henri. Pauchey stated, "Quiet elegance, which has always been the keynote to Fenway hospitality, will be preserved."[4] He anticipated an excellent season and an early full house.[5]

Fenway Pool Available to the Public

The Fenway pool was available to the public on a membership basis during the summers of 1957, 1958, and 1959. Membership for a family was $25 for the season, plus a 50-cent admission charge.

Use of the shuffleboard courts and tennis courts were included in the membership. Dressing rooms were available in the quarters over the garage, along with showers for both men and women. The pool was open through Labor Day.[6,7]

The Thirty-First Season Opened

The 31st season of the Fenway started on Friday, January 3, 1958. Extensive remodeling took place during the summer months that included the addition of 13 new bathrooms and new carpeting.

Sunday night buffets were held in the large dining room. Featured at the buffets were centerpieces of the ice carved figures, created by Chef Ed Taras.

Activities for hotel guests included weekly movies and a bridge night.[8]

Private Club Unsuccessful

For three years the Pauchets tried to make the Fenway into a private club, but it failed. Dunedin residents were invited to join, but not enough residents could afford it.[9]

In November, 1959, the Paucheys leased the Fenway Hotel to Richard C. Blair.[10]

St. Petersburg Times, December 31, 1957

Chapter 6

Richard Blair Introduces a Lifetime Residency Program

1959-1961

On November 12, 1959, the *St. Petersburg Times* announced that Richard C. Blair, President of Blair Enterprises, Inc. would lease the Fenway Hotel with an option to buy.

Blair was a graduate of Cornell University in Ithaca, New York and majored in hotel administration.[1] He was from Charleston, West Virginia, had worked as Assistant Manager of the Drake Hotel in Chicago for five years, and then managed the University of Chicago Faculty Club for five years.[2]

Blair arrived in Dunedin in September of 1959 and began managing the hotel on October 1st. He planned to keep the hotel open year-round.[2]

The growing economy in the Dunedin area and the new causeway to two offshore islands (Honeymoon and Caladesi Islands) were reasons for him to lease the hotel. Blair felt that the hotel could be used for spring and summer conventions. The dining room, sun parlor, and cocktail lounge were open to permanent residents of the area.[3]

What's What in Clearwater
February, 1960

Events Held at the Fenway

Blair wanted civic organizations and residents of the Clearwater-Dunedin area to use the hotel. He wanted the public to feel that the Fenway was their hotel.[1]

On Monday evening, December 29, 1959, he hosted a cocktail party attended by approximately 300 guests from the Tampa Bay area.[4]

A New Year's party, held on December 31, 1959, was the formal opening of the hotel. Nearly 200 guests attended the gala dinner and champagne buffet.[4]

Edward H. Hunt, Southeastern Director for the Jack Tar hotel chain, said, "The entire Tampa Bay area will benefit from the reopening of the Fenway. We, of the Jack Tar chain, recognize in Richard Blair, a hotel executive of top flight ability. Dunedin has long needed a year-round hotel of highest caliber and Mr. Blair has achieved that objective."[4]

Blair Enterprises, Inc. Purchased the Fenway

On July 7, 1960, newspapers announced that Blair Enterprises, Inc. purchased the Fenway Hotel and adjoining property on Edgewater Drive. The purchase price was not made public.

During the summer months air conditioning was added to the lounge, lobby, and dining room areas.[5]

The Fenway Club was organized and consisted of 200 family memberships. It was the social center for the community. Club members had the use of the pool, tennis courts and 18-hole putting green. Bridge parties, evening cookouts, and dinner dances were held for members twice a month.[6]

Lifetime Residency Program

Beginning October 1, 1960, forty rooms and suites were available for permanent residents to live at the Fenway year-round.[7] It was called a "Lifetime Residency Program" or "Retirement Plan of the Fenway Hotel". It was enthusiastically received. Several programs were sold. Cornell Industries, Inc.

(Orangeburg, New York) was the first to purchase this plan for its retiring president.[8]

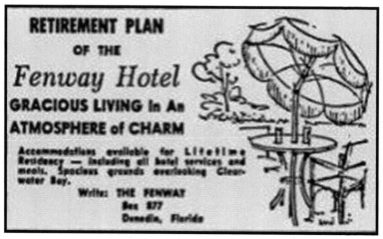

St. Petersburg Times, November 7, 1960

This program was intended for retired persons. Daily maid service, chauffeured car service, private nurses and companions were available. A registered nurse lived at the hotel. Three meals a day were included and each meal offered a variety of food items. Special diets were available.

Mr. Blair stated, "There is an increasing demand for this type of hotel service to meet the needs of our Senior Citizens who are eager to not have the burden of maintaining a private residence."[7]

According to this ad, published in the October 30, 1960 *Sarasota Herald-Tribune*, the Retirement Plan cost $275/month per person.

RETIREMENT PLAN of the Fenway Hotel

Gracious living in an atmosphere of charm. Accommodations available for lifetime residency, including all hotel services and meals at $275.00 monthly, per person. Spacious grounds overlooking Clearwater Bay WRITE . . .

THE FENWAY HOTEL

P.O. Box 877   Dunedin, Florida

All Florida-TV Week Magazine 10-30-60   9

Sarasota Herald-Tribune, October 30, 1960

New Owner for the Fenway

Unfortunately, Richard C. Blair wasn't able to make the Fenway financially successful. Dr. Bill W. Lanpher, in his book, "He is Able," said the Fenway was rescued from "financial doom" when it was purchased in June, 1961.[8]

The Fenway was purchased for $250,000 by the Fenway Academy, Inc. The Academy was closely associated with Trinity College and eventually the Fenway Hotel became the fourth campus for the College.[9]

Duncan Hines Vacation Guide Recognized the Fenway

The Duncan Hines Vacation Guide recognized the Fenway Hotel in its 16th printing, published in 1961. The book listed "good places to spend an enjoyable vacation." [10]

DUNEDIN (Pop. 8,304). 13 Mi. W. of Tampa. Rt. 19A.

19A—**Resort Hotel: Fenway.** Edgewater Drive, overlooking St. Joseph's Bay. 100 rooms. TV, cocktail lounge. Putting green, swimming pool, fishing. A fine resort hotel, nicely furnished. Amer. Plan SWB $18-$28; 2WB $28-$38. Suites $42-$48. No pets. Res. req. Jan.-March. Tel. 81-5011.

The Duncan Hines Vacation Guide

Chapter 7

Trinity College Turns the Fenway into a Campus

1961-1988

Dr. William T. Watson was the founder of the school that eventually became Trinity College. The school began with a dream of preparing men and women to work in the gospel ministry. "Trinity College was born in an environment of faith and prayer. From its commencement the seal of God's approval rested in an obvious way upon the work."[1]

Watson was born on May 21, 1901, and lived on a small farm near Lumberton, North Carolina. At the age of 14, he felt God's call to enter full time Christian service. At age 16, he entered Toccoa Falls Institute in Toccoa Falls, Georgia. That is where he began preaching and conducting summer tent revivals.

He graduated from Toccoa Falls Institute and spent a year in Nyaak, New York, at the Missionary Training Institute. He was then asked to come to St. Petersburg, Florida to start a church. In 1924, he founded the St. Petersburg Gospel Tabernacle.[1]

St. Petersburg Gospel Tabernacle

In 1924, Dr. Watson founded the St. Petersburg Gospel Tabernacle. The Tabernacle served as a beginning for Trinity College. Many people believe that if there hadn't been a Gospel Tabernacle there would not be a Trinity College.[1]

Beginning of an Educational Institute

While serving as pastor of the Tabernacle, Dr. Watson dreamed of starting a school to train Christian workers. The *Florida Fundamental Bible Institute* was started in 1932. The name changed to the *Florida Bible Institute*, then was renamed the *Florida Bible Institute and Seminary*. In 1947, a four-year college named *Trinity College* was started and was operated by the Institute.[2]

The school had three locations before the Fenway was purchased: Temple Terrace (1932-1943), St. Petersburg (1943-1950), and Belleair (1951-1969).

First Campus (1932-1943)
119 N Glen Arven Avenue, Temple Terrace, Florida

Dr. Watson was constantly looking for an appropriate location to start a school. One day he was visiting with Rev. Judson Wheeler Van DeVenter in Temple Terrace, Florida. They passed a beautiful, vacant hotel building owned by August Heckscher, from New York. The building was once the Club Morocco. Both Dr. Watson and Rev. Van DeVenter thought it would make a good Bible school.[1]

Since Dr. Watson didn't have money to purchase property, he didn't contact the owner. Two weeks later, an unsolicited telegram was delivered to him letting him know the owner would be at Temple Terrace the next day.[1]

When Dr. Watson met with Mr. Heckscher, he was asked if he was interested in the property. If he was interested, Heckscher gave him these terms – the property would be deeded to the school, no down payment, and no interest. The first payment would be due in ten years. The school would only have to pay expenses and upkeep.[1]

At the time, the owner was paying $7,000 a year in taxes plus custodial care for the empty building. Since the school would be a non-profit religious corporation, it would be tax exempt. Having the school use the building was a win, win situation for both Heckscher and the school.[3]

Florida Bible Institute Began

Dr. Watson quickly accepted this offer, formed a new board, and got the school ready for classes. Thirty students began taking classes at the *Florida Fundamental Bible Institute* in September, 1932. The first graduation was held in May, 1934.[1]

Billy Graham Attended the Institute

Billy Graham was a student at the Temple Terrace campus. He came from Charlotte, North Carolina, in January 1937 and graduated in 1940. Earlier he had attended Bob Jones College in Cleveland, Tennessee. Billy recalled that he was very frightened to talk and could say only three or four sentences.

He came down with the flu and returned home. He had a slow recovery, so the family doctor suggested a warmer climate for him. He learned about the *Florida Bible Institute* and loved the idea of palm trees, fresh grapefruit, and that the school was on the edge of a golf course. The school's

open curriculum appealed to him as it gave him more time
to study the Bible and learn to preach.[4]

Class of 1940. Billy Graham is third from right, back row.
Source: *1972 Trinity College Yearbook*

His Christian commitment grew at the Institute, and
he had many opportunities to preach on street corners and
at small rural churches. He preached to the people who
came into the Franklin Street Mission in Tampa.[5]

His first preaching assignment was at the Tampa
Municipal Trailer Park. Trinity students preached at trailer
parks in the area as part of their studies.

His first radio address was broadcast on WSUN. He
asked people to pray for him because his knees were
knocking. For a few months he served as Assistant Pastor at
the Gospel Tabernacle in St. Petersburg.[3]

Graham received his calling to the ministry in North
Carolina. He received his calling for evangelism on the
nearby Florida golf course. One night he was pacing on the

18th hole and finally said, "All right, Lord, if you want me, you've got me.[5]

At Graham's graduation, Vera G. Resue, the valedictorian said that the time was ripe for another Luther, Wesley, or Moody. The class did not realize, at the time, that one of their fellow graduates would become a world-renowned speaker and preach the gospel throughout the world.[4]

When Billy Graham graduated in 1940, the school did not grant degrees, just diplomas, so he continued his education at Wheaten College in Illinois.[3]

Second Campus (1943-1950)
3151 Tangerine Avenue, St. Petersburg, Florida

Since gasoline was rationed during World War II, it was difficult for Dr. Watson and the staff to get back and forth to the Temple Terrace campus. Since the lease at Temple Terrace had expired, the Institute wanted to find something closer to home. In 1943 officials of the school relocated the institute to a new campus on Tangerine Avenue in St. Petersburg.[3]

Announcement of New College

The founding of a four-year college was announced at graduation exercises held on May 5, 1946. This new college was named Trinity College and would be operated by the Institute. Both schools would have the same executive board.[6]

Third Campus (1951-1970)
100 Coe Road, Belleair, Florida

On January 17, 1951, *The Evening Independent* reported that Trinity College had purchased the Belleair Country Inn and would turn it from "roulette to religion." Dr. Watson purchased the 54-room building and 4½ acres on Clearwater Harbor for more than $100,000.[7]

The College moved in immediately. The present building was remodeled and an administration building was built. The great ballroom became a chapel and a lounge for the students. The cocktail bars served plain water. One bar became a sandwich bar and one became a reading room.[7]

Fourth Campus (1961-1988)
Fenway Hotel 453 Edgewater Drive, Dunedin, Florida

By 1960, Trinity College had outgrown the Belleair campus and the Fenway was for sale. The Fenway campus was purchased before the Belleair location was debt free.[1]

Billy Graham realized that there was lack of space when he visited the Belleair campus. He promised $10,000 when the time came to move. Graham was in England when the hotel was purchased.

Dr. Watson said, "The hotel was worth $1 million, but was being sold for a quarter of that price. I wrote the contract by hand on a single piece of paper and sealed it with personal check for $500."[3]

Graham's office sent $2,000, and Watson raised the rest of the $10,000 down payment. When Graham returned to the U.S. he sent the school 1,000 chairs and promised another $5,000 for classroom expansion.[3]

Hotel Became Fenway Academy

A headline in the June 30, 1961 edition of the *St. Petersburg Times* said, "Fenway Hotel Changes Hands, Will Be Academy." The Academy was a co-educational school and taught Christian principles to students in grades 8th through 12th.[8]

It was announced in August 3, 1963, the Fenway Academy would become a Bible college preparatory school and enrollment would be limited to students in grades 10, 11, and 12.[9]

During this time, the Fenway campus was used by both Trinity College and the Fenway Academy. The women from both schools were housed in the Fenway Hotel. The

Academy boys were housed in Pilgrim Hall (2-story building in back of the hotel) and the Trinity College men were housed on the campus in Belleair.[9]

Billy Graham's 25th Anniversary of His Graduation

Billy Graham arrived Friday, January 22, 1965 to observe the 25th anniversary of his graduation from Trinity College. He stayed at the Fenway until Sunday. He spoke at a banquet for Trinity students and faculty members at the Jack Tar Harrison Hotel on Saturday.

Dr. Graham was class president of the Class of 1940. Other class officers and members sat with him at the head of the table. At the time Graham was on the Advisory Board of the college.[10]

Pilgrim Hall Dorm for Male Students
Source: *1976-1977 Trinity College Yearbook*

Auditorium on the Campus

At the May 15, 1966 graduation, Dr. Watson said that he hoped to hold graduation next year in a new 750 seat, air-conditioned auditorium. Construction began summer and fall (1966) on the $200,000 building.[11]

An article in 1969 told that the building that housed the auditorium also had rooms that featured a Billy Graham Hall of Evangelism, a rare Bible Museum, and a Sacred Music Hall of Fame. Displayed in the Hall of Evangelism were parts of the Billy Graham exhibition that was at the 1964 New York World's Fair along with a life size painting of The Last Supper.[12]

Auditorium Complex
Source: *1976-1977 Trinity College Yearbook*

Selling of the Belleair Campus

By 1969, the Belleair campus was being used mostly for seminary classes. Trinity wanted to sell that campus and move all college work to the Dunedin campus, as the facilities at the Dunedin campus had been expanded to allow for this.[13]

In March of 1970, the Town Commission rezoned the Trinity College Belleair property so it could be sold for multi-family buildings. Once the zoning was changed Mann Associates purchased the property and condos were built on the land.[14]

Special Birthday Banquet for Dr. Watson

In July, 1977, a 75th birthday banquet was arranged by the College Alumni Association for Dr. Watson. More than 800 persons attended. Many more wanted to attend but couldn't because of lack of space.

The speaker was Dr. Billy Graham who gave his appreciation to Dr. Watson and to Trinity College for what it did for him. Graham told the audience that memories were flooding his heart. He honored Dr. Watson and others who built their lives into his when he was a student on campus.[1]

Staff Photo
St. Petersburg Times, January 28, 1974

Trinity College's Founder Passed Away

In July, 1980, Dr. Watson became ill, but continued to preach and teach students to "preach Jesus." He was sustained by his tremendous will to work for the Lord.

On June 5, 1981 Dr. Watson passed away and "the Lord welcomed him home." Dr. Watson left a great legacy to carry on the principles of Christian education, "training young people for practical Christian service." [15]

Dr. William T. Watson

Trinity Looked to Move from Dunedin

As early as 1984, there was talk that Trinity College was looking to relocate the college from Dunedin. Their board of directors discussed building a new campus but had not found a suitable location.

On May 22, 1985, Dean Barry Banther, told the *Suncoast News* that "serious negotiations" were going on that would move the college to Tarpon Springs. He said that they had outgrown the Fenway campus and their growth had been limited by the lack of facilities.[16]

There was excitement among Trinity officials, faculty, and students about a brand-new facility, since all their campuses had been second-hand properties. Banther said that the school had thrived on second-hand properties and had always been thankful for what God had given them.[17]

Trinity Moved to Pasco County

When Trinity left Dunedin, the faculty and students felt that, even with the city's growth and change, Dunedin residents gave them a strong sense of community. The new and larger campus in Pasco County would allow more students to attend Trinity. The Dunedin campus had become too small, and the cost of maintaining the buildings too expensive.[18]

The last graduation on the Dunedin Campus was held in May, 1988.

Fifth Campus (1988-Present)
2430 Welbilt Boulevard, New Port Richey, Florida

In August, 1985, a gift of 20 acres of land from Dr. James P. Gills, was accepted by officials of Trinity College. The property was valued at $2 million and was known as Mitchell Ranch. Dr. Gills, land developer and well-known eye surgeon, gave another 20 acres in 2002 to make room for growth.[19]

The *Clearwater Sun* reported that "Trinity College is moving to Pasco County, but the fate of one of Dunedin's most cherished landmarks is still up in the air."[20]

Fenway Property Empty

Trinity left the Dunedin campus in 1988 and moved to the Pasco campus. No one realized how difficult it would be to sell the Fenway property and how long it would remain empty.

Commencement Exercises
Year Unknown, Source: *1972 Trinity Yearbook*

THE FENWAY HOTEL

Chapter 8

What to Do with the Fenway?

1988-1991

The Trinity College Board of Trustees tried hard to sell the Fenway property before they moved but were unable to do so. There was a couple from Sherman Oaks, California, who purchased the property soon after Trinity moved in 1988, but their plans for the Fenway did not work out.

The following are some of the ideas proposed for the hotel:

Dunedin City Hall

The City of Dunedin looked at the property in March of 1985 to see if they should move City Hall offices there. At the time, City Hall offices were located in three separate buildings. That meant time was wasted because staff had to go from building to building to get work accomplished. John Lawrence, Dunedin City Manager, toured the facility and said "It's enormous. It could accommodate all the city staff."[1]

A task force to study this possibility was appointed by the commissioners. It included an architect, a contractor, an engineer and a banker. It was determined that major renovations were needed and the cost of the property and renovation of the buildings would cost more than $6.5 million. Purchase of the land with intent to demolish and construct a new city hall would cost around $4.14 million.[2]

They "advised the city not to consider the site for anything but a park."[3]

Townhouse/Condo Units

In December of 1985, a developer from Tarpon Springs, Emmanuel Tsavaris, submitted an application to rezone the use of the property. He wanted to build three five-story buildings (a total of 105 units) and 28 townhouse units that would bring the total units to 133.

To comply with a new city ordinance on gross density, the developer had to create a revised plan with fewer units. The Dunedin Planning and Zoning Board discussed the site plan at their meeting on January 9, 1986.[4] A purchase contract was signed contingent on the zoning change.

The city commissioners voted to not allow 110 condominium units to be built on the site. They turned down the zoning request to change the land-use from public/semi-public to high-density residential. Neighbors who lived near the property applauded the board's decision.[5]

Blue Jays Baseball Team

Another suggestion was for the Toronto Blue Jays to purchase the hotel. The Toronto Blue Jays baseball team held their spring training in Dunedin. Some players and staff purchased homes in the area, most rented apartments, stayed in private homes, or rented rooms at a hotel.[6]

The Blue Jays were interested in looking at the property but felt the $3 million asking price was too high. In March, 1987, the Blue Jays decided they were not interested in purchasing the Fenway. They didn't have the money and, in order to pay off the property, they would have to operate the hotel year-round and they were not interested in doing this.[7]

Trinity College to Develop a Retirement Center

Before Trinity College moved, they wondered if they should develop the property themselves. They considered opening a "life care center" to house elderly residents. The Trinity College Board of Trustees decided to explore building condominiums for the elderly.[8]

A meeting of neighbors was held at the Dunedin Library in November of 1987 where plans were presented. Ellerbe Inc., a Tampa consulting firm, was hired to design the project.

There was a small group of investors who emphasized to residents that the investors would not go forward without neighborhood support. Martin Bakke, who put the development group together, said – "If the homeowners of the neighborhood don't approve the project, it ends there."[9]

The Ellerbe plan showed the retirement center, made up of 180 to 200 apartments in a three-story building. A staff of 30 would run the center. The main college building would be preserved and used mainly as a meeting area. The new portion would be built behind the hotel and would not be seen from Edgewater Drive.[9]

Couple Bought the Fenway to Be a Retirement Center

On April 28, 1988 a headline in the *St. Petersburg Times* read "Trinity College Sells Waterfront Property."

John and Darlene Van Harlingen, from Sherman Oaks, California, planned to operate a retirement center and use the same plan prepared by Ellerbe, Inc. that Trinity College presented at the November, 1987 meeting with residents of the neighborhood.

Before they could begin remodeling the Fenway, the city would have to change the land-use designation of the property. A rezoning application was filed with the city in May of 1988.[10]

Homeowners in the neighborhood were supportive of a retirement center, but they wanted to see the designs to make sure no major changes were made. Residents didn't want the proposed retirement center to become a rental apartment complex.[10]

John and Darlene Van Harlingen paid more than $1.6 million for the property. The offer came right before the 1988 graduation was held on the campus, and right before Trinity moved to Pasco County.[11]

The owners planned to apply for the Fenway Hotel to be placed on the National Register of Historic Places. Historical experts were hired to research the hotel's past. They felt the building qualified for this register for several reasons, one being its association with Trinity College.[12]

Fenway for Sale Again

In October, 1988, John and Darlene Van Harlingen put the Fenway site up for sale. The owners asked $3.5 million for the property which was twice what they paid for it.[13]

The reason they gave for selling was they were having difficulty getting approval from the city to build a retirement center. The zoning staff recommended not having a retirement center there because it was inappropriate for the area.[14]

The City Commissioners met in November of 1988 and rejected the proposal that the Fenway be turned into a retirement center. The commissioners voted 5-0 against the land-use amendment and zoning changes.[15]

More Suggestions

An art center was suggested. The idea of using the Fenway as City Hall came up again in 1988. A joint center for various organizations was suggested.

The real-estate agent trying to sell the property said that "the property's zoning makes it impossible to do anything on the site. The city isn't leaving anyone any alternatives."[16] The zoning of the property only allowed for a school, church or hospital to occupy the building.

Mayor Koutsourais was quoted as saying "That piece of property is the most unique in the whole city of Dunedin. I'm really hoping there will be some better ideas".[16]

A Luxury Hotel

December of 1988, a local developer, Donald (William) Fry, wanted to do a $20,000 study to see if a it would be financially feasible to convert the "Mediterranean-style mansion into a 120-room luxury hotel."[17]

On February 3, 1989, the *St. Petersburg Times* reported that Donald Fry had discontinued the study and was pulling out of the project. Fry said that there was a lack of communication between his company and the property's owners, John and Darlene Van Harlingen.[18]

Sell a Portion of the Land to the City

In February of 1989, John and Darlene Van Harlingen offered to sell a portion of the property to the city for $1.4 million. They proposed that the city buy the buildings on the property behind the hotel and gain the waterfront. The city would need no down payment but would pay the Van Harlingen's $12,000-a-month mortgage payments to Trinity College. The buildings they offered were the 300-seat auditorium, administration building with a library, building with classrooms, and a rental house. John Lawrence pointed out, "This is not a very attractive deal for the city. We'd be taking over their note and we'd not be getting the main building."[19]

Foreclosure Filed

An article in the September 28, 1989 *St. Petersburg Times* reported that John and Darlene Van Harlingen had not made a payment on the mortgage to Trinity College since December, 1988, and owed $1.39 million for the principal, interest, late charges, and title search expense.

A foreclosure lawsuit was filed in Pinellas-Pasco Circuit Court. Trinity College, Peoples State Bank, and AmeriBank sued John and Darlene Van Harlingen. Trinity College needed the money so they could finish their new campus.[20]

Van Harlingen's and Trinity College Sued

In November of 1989, the Van Harlingen's and Trinity College became embroiled in litigation. Trinity College sued John and Darlene Van Harlingen for a $1.6 million mortgage foreclosure. The couple filed a countersuit claiming that the college knew that the project for a retirement home would fail.

"They indicated that there would be no problem in getting a zoning change" said Joseph Kalish, an attorney for the owners.[21]

Two More Lawsuits

December of 1989 brought two more lawsuits. An architect sued Trinity College for not being paid for work for the Pasco County campus. Trinity wasn't able to pay this because of the $1.4 million foreclosure suit against the purchasers of the property in Dunedin.[22]

The other lawsuit was from Ellerbe Becket Architects and Engineers. They alleged that they had a contract with the owners of the hotel property, John and Darlene Van Harlingen, to create a site plan and serve as a liaison between them and the community. They were owed $14,634 in damages, plus interest from October 24, 1989, and legal fees.[23]

Finally - A New Owner for the Fenway

Good news came in early 1990. A suitable buyer for the Fenway property was found.

The Fenway was saved and the future of this famous landmark in Dunedin looked promising!!

Note:

After they sold the hotel, John and Darlene Van Harlingen sued the city of Dunedin in November of 1990. They asked for more than $50,000 in damages. They said while they were purchasing the Trinity College property, the city told them they would be allowed to build a retirement center.

They believed that after the land was purchased, the city changed the zoning to keep them from doing this. They claimed these ordinances caused a severe economic loss to them and they were forced to sell the property under duress.[24]

Chapter 9

Schiller International University's First Campus in the United States

1991-2006

In the late 1980s and early 1990s, Dr. Walter Leibrecht was searching for a location to start a campus of Schiller International University (SUI) in the United States. There were already Schiller campuses in: Germany, Spain, England, Switzerland, and two campuses in France.

Dr. Leibrecht had looked at locations in Vermont, California, Orlando, and Boston when a friend told him about a place for sale in Dunedin, Florida, that would make an ideal location for the university.

When he saw the Fenway property, he knew this is where he wanted to open his new campus. Dr. Leibrecht said, "When I first saw this place, I thought, what a wonderful building to start a school in. It is aesthetically pleasing and directly on the waterfront. It is an unusual combination." He went on to say, "This will be a perfect place for people new in the United States. It is close to a metropolitan area, but here you have a quiet atmosphere, water and sunshine."[1]

Dr. Walter Leibrecht

In the early 1950s, Dr. Leibrecht completed his Doctorate degree from Heidelberg University. He was chosen to come to the United States to teach. He was a professor and respected scholar for 10 years at Columbia, Harvard and the University of Chicago.

He became interested in the American approach to education that developed the individual student, gave academic choice, and offered a curriculum that was relevant for the modern world. American students could meet with their professors and receive advice from them.

He loved his home country of Germany and wanted to share this educational approach in his home country. He developed an idea of offering programs for Americans in Europe.[2] The college was very successful and many universities in the United States chose Schiller as their study abroad venue in Germany.

Schiller's First Campus

Dr. Leibrecht saved $100,000 and persuaded banks to lend him four times that amount to start the first campus. In 1964, he started Schiller College in a 16th Century castle in Ingersheim, near Heidelberg, Germany.[2]

The college was named Schiller in honor of Friedrich von Schiller, an influential German philosopher, poet, playwright, and historian, who was an inspiration to Dr. Leibrecht.[2]

Schiller started with 25 students, mostly Americans living in Europe. Dr. Leibrecht was quoted as saying "I wanted to establish a small, independent university, offering students high-quality education where close attention to each student would inspire them and help them develop self-confidence."[2]

Schiller Expanded to Other Countries

Dr. Leibrecht started campuses in other countries because he wanted students to have an opportunity to live and study in different cultures without losing course credits. He realized the importance of having students from different nationalities studying side by side at the same school. Classes at Schiller were taught in English so Americans could study in Europe without knowing a second language. [2]

Twenty-five students registered in 1964, and by the early 1970s, the number of students increased to 1500. By 1966 the programs outgrew the first campus and expanded to other settings. Full degree programs were added to their study abroad opportunities.

In 1969, campuses opened in Paris and Madrid, and the German college had moved to Heidelberg. By 1973, additional campuses in London and Strasbourg opened.[2]

Attending Schiller, students could transfer among the campuses as they earned credits towards a degree. They could study and socialize with students from different countries. When they graduated, they had established a global network and an understanding of the different cultures they would encounter during their professional careers.[3]

In 1981, Schiller College became Schiller International University and in 1983, Schiller was accredited by the Association of Independent Colleges and Schools (AICS).[3]

Purchasing the Fenway

The *St. Petersburg Times* on January 24, 1990 reported – "An international university may make its home at the former Trinity College site, which could end the controversy over the proper use of the 68-year-old landmark on Edgewater Drive."[4]

A zoning exception and agreeing on a price with owners, John and Darlene Van Harlingen, was needed. A purchase agreement was reached and the zoning restored back to "institutional" to allow an educational institution to be on the property. The purchase price was reported to be $1.4 million.[5]

The end of February, 1990, the Dunedin Board of Adjustment and Appeals unanimously made a ruling and granted the variance of special exception to the Fenway Hotel. This meant that the university was approved. Dunedin residents gathered at a meeting at City Hall and gave a huge ovation after this ruling was announced.[6]

On March 1, 1990 the deal was finalized, the contract signed, and the Fenway Hotel would be known as the Dunedin Campus of Schiller International University.[7]

Getting Ready for Students

The campus needed to get ready for students so plans were made quickly. First, the roof needed to be repaired and a termite problem eliminated. Over the first three years, approximately $1 million was spent on renovations and equipment.[8]

The plumbing - almost 65 years old - hadn't had much work done to it. The boiler system needed to be replaced. The swimming pool was washed with acid and filled.

Dozens of windows were repaired because of termite damage to the wood frames.[8]

Fifty-two rooms needed to be ready for students. The remaining 44 rooms would be shut off until the university enrolled more students. Contractors fixed the library, administration offices, and classrooms.[8]

People who looked at the Fenway said, – "if the building had gone another two years it would have been too far gone; it would have cost too much to restore."[9]

Students Arrived on Campus

Students began taking classes on the Dunedin campus in January of 1991. About 50 students from Schiller's campuses in France, Great Britain, Spain, Germany, and Switzerland were expected to finish their junior and senior years in the United States.[10]

Schiller hired local faculty. Twelve faculty members were part-time. Some faculty were already teaching at the University of Tampa or St. Petersburg Junior College.[10]

The first students attending classes on the Schiller Dunedin campus included 26 students from 13 countries. At the end of the semester these students gave the campus high marks and eighteen of these students planned to return in the fall when classes resumed.[11]

Dunedin Residents Welcomed Schiller

There was much interest once news was announced that the university was coming to Dunedin. Dr. Leibrecht received calls from local residents asking him to lecture and from people who wanted to be part of the faculty.[6]

Dunedin residents took Schiller students on tours of the area and became involved in other ways with Schiller and its students.

Friends of the Library

A group called Schiller Friends of the Library was organized by the first librarian, Janis Coker, to raise money to help the library grow. The public was invited to become involved. The costs of annual memberships were: $10 individual membership, $15 family, $25 business, and $5 student.

Schiller International University,
Dunedin Campus Library,
cordially invites you
to an organizational meeting
to initiate the
Friends of the Library.

7:30 p.m., Wednesday
January 9, 1991,
the meeting will be held in the
Schiller International University Library,
453 Edgewater Drive Dunedin
second floor, Administration Building.

Invitation to join Friends of the Library
January 9, 1991

The Purpose of the Friends of Schiller Library was to "establish a group of interested people - - local residents, alumni, faculty, students, staff and other supporters of SIU – to reach out into the larger community with programs and projects that contribute to the purposes of the university and enhance the cultural and educational resources of the area." [12]

Book sales were held on the front porch of the hotel in the fall and spring. Those attending the book sale were invited to go into the lobby and see the hotel. Tours of the campus were arranged by special request.

Besides book sales there were programs and musical events sponsored by the Friends of the Library. Programs were presented by faculty and administrators of the University, speakers from the Dunedin community, and speakers brought in from outside the community. Dunedin residents were invited to attend.[12]

Schillerbrations

One annual fundraising event sponsored by the Friends of the Library was called a Schillerbration. The annual Schillerbrations were held near the November 10th birthday of Friedrich Schiller, the namesake of the University. This event was held so the Dunedin community could become acquainted with the university while helping the Library.

The first Schillerbration was held Saturday, November 10, 1991. It consisted of a luncheon of German cuisine and black forest cake for dessert. A program of German music was performed and Schiller students presented readings from Schiller's poetry.

A total of eight Schillerbrations were held. The last one was held on Saturday, November 8, 1998.[12]

Schillerbration

SCHILLERBRATION I
SCHILLER INTERNATIONAL UNIVERSITY DUNEDIN CAMPUS

November 10, 1991

REGISTRATION - NAME TAGS

Please be seated in the Dining Hall

Introductory remarks by Master of Ceremonies John Lawrence
Dunedin City Manager

MENU
Smoked pork chop baked in sauerkraut
Sauerbraten
Cooked red cabbage
Himmel und Erde (potatoes, apples and bacon)
Green beans, onions and bacon
Breads and rolls
Dessert: Black Forest Cake
Coffee, tea iced or hot, milk

Schiller Program and Menu
November 10, 1991

Dunedin Campus Began to Grow

In the fall of 1993, Schiller hoped to have an enrollment of 150-200 students. Nearly 50 countries were represented when Schiller began its third year on the Dunedin campus.

For most students, coming to the Dunedin campus was a continuation of studies from other Schiller campuses. For many students, this was their first time in the United States. [13]

Schiller Headquarters Moved to Dunedin

In 1994, the University moved their headquarters from Germany to Dunedin. At least three high-level officers and the President of the University, Dr. Leibrecht, moved to Dunedin. It meant that Schiller had to show its financial resources to the state, keep student records here, and become registered as a corporation in the United States.[14]

Activities for Students

There were many activities planned for students. One activity was the annual International Food Festival.

Teams of students worked together to make recipes from their home countries. Serving tables were decorated and students wore clothing from their home countries. Dunedin residents were invited to attend this colorful and delicious event.

A popular event for students was the annual bus trip to Disney World in Orlando. Many local activities were planned for students such as dinners, sporting events, concerts, and other activities the students were interested in. Transportation to the Countryside Mall and other popular shopping areas was offered.

Not every student lived in the hotel. Some rented rooms from neighbors, lived in apartments in Dunedin, or apartments in surrounding areas. Some apartments were furnished, but some were not. Students often had to buy furniture and furnishings for their apartments and would purchase items from graduating students who were moving away.

If they did not own a car, or knew someone who owned a car, public transportation was used to get around.

Model United Nations

Schiller students began participating the Model United Nations in 1995. This competition was designed for college and university students to recreate what it was like to be involved in the United Nations. Every year students were given the name of a country and were to learn as much as they could about this country.

Students debated and discussed topics and decided how the United Nations should respond. Delegates sat at tables and had the flag of the country they represented in front of them. Name tags were raised when they wanted to be recognized to talk. They followed the same rules as the United Nations. One example was a set time limit (about 2 minutes) for each speaker.

Some of the reasons students were involved in the Model United Nations were: it prepared them to work in international relations, they learned a lot about the countries, and they wanted to see how closely their decisions matched those of the real United Nations.[15]

Dunedin residents were invited to a free demonstration on March 22, 1995. This helped students prepare for the competition in New York City.[16]

On April 10-15, 1995, students from all over the world gathered at the United Nations General Assembly Hall in New York. This was the 50th anniversary of the United Nations.

The country assigned to the Schiller group in 1995 was Chad, a country in Central Africa. Five Schiller students competed with 1,800 students from around the world.[16]

Schiller students participated in the Model United Nations from 1995 to 2010. Other locations they traveled to compete were Atlanta, Georgia and Bethune Cookman University in Dayton Beach, Florida.

Dr. Jeff Maddux, the Model UN Coordinator at Schiller, said, "In New York we competed against over 2000 students from over 200 universities from more than two dozen countries and were often joined by students from other SIU campuses." He reported that some of the former Schiller Model UN students currently work for the UN, the EU, or their country's Foreign Ministry.

Edgewater Room - Fine Dining

Starting in fall, 2003, a casual fine dining experience for the Dunedin and Schiller community was offered twice a month at the University. Students in the college's School of Tourism and Hospitality program worked in the kitchen to prepare food under the direction of campus Chef, Paul Kennedy.

This experience gave students a hands-on learning experience and practical knowledge of the hospitality industry. Prices were relatively low because all they needed to do was to break even and not make a profit. Students in the program from all over the world, worked together, and had a good time doing so.[17]

Schiller Academy

The Schiller Academy, a high school program, opened in 1997 with eight juniors and seniors. Classes were held in the auditorium building located behind the hotel. Enrollment doubled by spring.

In the fall, 1998, Schiller started a four-year high school program. Sixty to seventy freshmen and sophomores were expected the first year, three-fourths being from foreign countries.

Schiller Academy students from the United States could attend other Schiller campuses that had high schools.[18]

The Effect of September 11, 2001 on Schiller

The horrifying event on September 11, 2001 had a huge impact on the number of students coming to the United States to study at American colleges and universities. It became more difficult for students to obtain visas to come to this country. Because the majority of students attending the Dunedin campus came from foreign countries, enrollment at the campus was affected.

There was an 11% drop in enrollment at the Dunedin campus which meant a decrease in revenue to the school. Plans for hiring extra staff and expanding programs were delayed.

Eventually, getting student visas became less of a problem allowing the Dunedin campus to continue to grow, but it meant that the university had to keep a more watchful eye on students that came to study on Schiller's Dunedin campus.[19]

Schiller Sold the Fenway – Moved to a New Location

After recognizing that major renovations needed to be completed on the buildings, and rising insurance costs, the school decided to look for another location. Properties in Dunedin, Clearwater, and Largo were considered.

In February of 2006, the 6.4-acre Fenway property was sold to George Rahdert who planned to restore the hotel back to an elegant historic hotel. He paid $8 million for the land and buildings.[20]

In April of 2006, the former Hospice of the Florida Suncoast property at 300 East Bay Drive in Largo was purchased by Schiller for $3.5 million. Much construction work was needed on the Largo property, so the University could not move right away.

While they were renovating their new campus in Largo, Schiller leased the Dunedin campus from George Rahdert.

Schiller moved to Largo in August 2006, and classes began that September.[21]

Schiller Founder Passed Away

Dr. Walter Leibrecht died of heart failure on Saturday, February 24, 2007. He was survived by his wife of 51 years, Lydia; four sons, Thomas, Harald, Christoph, and Markus; a daughter, Bettina; and seven grandchildren.

He left behind a huge legacy that helped "thousands of individuals achieve success through his innovative educational opportunities."[22]

Dr. Walter Leibrecht

Looking Forward

It was exciting that the Fenway was sold to someone who appreciated how special it was. It was going to be interesting to watch the progress of the restoration of the Fenway.

Chapter 10

George Rahdert Plans to Restore the Fenway

2006-2013

This part of the Fenway story began full of promise, high hopes, and a dream to restore the Fenway Hotel back to its former glory. George Rahdert purchased the Fenway in 2006 and wanted to restore the hotel and make it into a combination hotel-condominium.

This idea began to fall apart and problems developed when he started planning the renovation.

Planning the Renovation

Rahdert had already participated in as many as 20 historic preservation projects in St. Petersburg, Florida. One of the first things he hoped to do was put the Fenway Hotel on the National Register of Historic Places and make it into a four-star hotel.[1]

The idea of renovating the building interested city officials, but site plans needed to be submitted before they could give permission to go ahead.[2] Rahdert would later say at a commission meeting, "I have fallen in love with your Fenway Hotel."[3]

Rahdert met with council members and some of their concerns were density, public access, and harmony with the neighborhood. If there were any concerns about preserving the building Rahdert said that he would exceed their expectations.[1]

He wanted to have a hotel-condominium where owners participated in a "leasing pool" with a second-phase hotel facility overlooking a courtyard, and residential townhouses to buffer the hotel from the neighborhood.

Rahdert was concerned about residents' input and said, "For this to work, it has to be something that provides a benefit to the public."[1]

It didn't take long for neighbors to give their input and it wasn't all positive.

Neighbors Opposed Plans

An editorial in the *St. Petersburg Times* April 20, 2006, said residents of Dunedin were happy with the purchase of the Fenway, but "their cheers turned to dismay as soon as Rahdert started talking about his plans for the property."[4]

Rahdert wanted to restore the hotel, but he imagined an upscale hotel resort like the Vinoy Hotel, in St. Petersburg, while residents wanted something on the order of a bed and breakfast, with lots of yard surrounding the beautifully restored building.

Rahdert was shocked by the opposition that occurred before a site plan was even presented to the city. His plan consisted of an "expanded 250-room, upscale hotel resort with fine dining, a day spa and a three-story parking garage."

Other changes were two four-story wings added to the hotel, widening Edgewater Drive and adding a crosswalk.

These plans were too much for some neighbors and they organized for a battle.[5]

Neighbors Hired an Attorney

In January 2006, thirty-five angry residents met to get organized for a battle. They discussed hiring an attorney to represent them. Some of the Edgewater Drive residents organized into a group called "Save Dunedin Neighborhoods."[5]

The neighborhood group hired a powerful land use attorney, Ed Armstrong. The attorney made it clear that legal obstacles had to be overcome in order to move forward with the resort hotel. One of these obstacles was changing the residential zoning to commercial use. He said that Rahdert's vision of the property was inconsistent with that of the neighbors, and it would be difficult to "bridge that gap." He predicted that it might take years to resolve the matter.[5]

The group of thirty-five who were against the plan soon expanded to hundreds from all parts of Dunedin, although there were some residents who felt that the project would be good for the city. Editorials began to be published in the St. Petersburg Times, both for and against the plans for the hotel. [6,7,8]

Rahdert Faced City Commission

At a city commission meeting in June of 2006, a unanimous decision was made to not enter into negotiations with Rahdert at that time. Issues listed were land use designation, number of proposed rooms, and neighborhood opposition. These issues needed to be addressed before any further approval would be given.

Dunedin Mayor Bob Hackworth told Rahdert that he could come back with a different proposal. [9]

New Architect, New Plan

Rahdert presented a new plan in November of 2006, using a new architect, Dunedin resident Roberto Sanchez. The proposed plan preserved the historic Fenway Hotel. All other buildings on the property would be torn down. The new plan proposed 150 rooms and no parking garage. [10]

Before the City Commission meeting in November, Rahdert and Sanchez met with neighbors and residents to explain the details of their new plan. He wanted their support with his new plan before he met with the city commission.

In the end, the commissioners voted 4-1 to enter into a development agreement with Rahdert, but said more work needed to be done on the plan. This didn't mean that the commission approved of the project, but meant they supported entering discussions on a possible development agreement. [11]

At the May 17, 2007 Commission meeting the City Commission signed off on the development plan for the Fenway. This came more than a year after his first proposal for the restoration of the Fenway Hotel had been presented to the City Commiision. [12]

A Compromise was Reached

It took time and hard work between Dunedin residents, officials, and the owner of the Fenway to find a compromise for the design of the Fenway Hotel. Rahdert spent a year working to fit his plan into what the residents and neighbors would accept.

Some of the compromises he made were to reduce the number of rooms to 150, eliminate a parking garage, add a wall around the property, modify the entrance and internal road network, and save most of the front lawn.[13]

Tentative Approval Given & Approval of Development Agreement

After hours of public debate, on March 5, 2009, the City Commission "gave tentative approval to renovate the existing Fenway Hotel to serve again as an exclusive hotel." This was a 5-part public hearing and dozens of residents spoke for and against the hotel.[14]

At the March 26, 2009 City Commission meeting a development agreement was approved for the Fenway. The hotel site plan was being revised and would come back to the Commission at a later date.[14]

George Rahdert's dream to restore the Fenway to its former glory was a major step closer. The building would be restored into the 1920s period. When completed, the hotel would have 132 rooms, a 151-seat restaurant, a 6,000-square-foot ballroom, 10,000-square-feet of meeting space, a spa, and retail shops.[15]

Final Approval Given

The City Commission gave their final approval in May, 2009 for Rahdert to begin renovations on the Fenway Hotel. Downtown merchants, the Chamber of Commerce, historical preservationists, and the City Commission were all supportive, but there still were neighbors who worried that the hotel would change their neighborhood.[16]

Rahdert planned to begin construction immediately. Private investors would back the project. The Integrity Hotel Group LLC would assist in the planning process. Rahdert said it would take between 18 months to two years for the restoration to be completed.[17]

He hoped that this hotel would entice tourists to shop in downtown Dunedin and go to the waterfront. There would be a shuttle to Caladesi Island. A health club and ice cream shop would be in the hotel and could be used by local residents.[18]

Financial Issues Announced

Everything was looking good until December 20, 2009. After almost four years of trying to get permission to renovate the Fenway, Rahdert announced that he didn't know where he was going to get the money to do so.

RBC Centura lenders, backed out of the project. They said it was because it took too long to get the project approved and they got tired of waiting.

Rahdert said, "In that period of time, the financial markets pretty much melted down. They (RBC Centura) gave up on the project and revoked their commitment for funding."[19]

After this financial setback, Rahdert had three alternatives: 1) find someone to buy him out, 2) secure full financing of $17-20 million to complete the project, or 3) secure less financing ($10 million) and build the project in stages, restore ballrooms, common spaces, and offer fine dining.[19]

In 2010, the bank that loaned Rahdert millions to restore the Fenway began foreclosure on the property. According to the lawsuit, in August of 2009 Rahdert "stopped payments on the bank loans and development costs."[20]

Online Auction of the Fenway

An online auction of the Fenway Hotel was announced in the St. Petersburg Times on March 2, 2012. The auction would be held on April 5, 2012. RBC Bank hoped to sell the property for $10.6 million, but Rahdert doubted it would sell for that much because records showed the property assessment was only $2 million.[21]

Over the years he had spent thousands of dollars to fix the property. Some of these costs included architectural planning, repairs, painting the outside, and lawn care.

He searched for another buyer, business partner or funding source. Rahdert still hoped a new buyer would preserve the hotel. He stated, "The bank is in the driver's seat, and it'll be potluck on who buys it. I hope that the party who buys the property will continue to make the effort to turn it into what it can be, which is a beautifully preserved historic building that will bring a high level of tourism and community opportunities to the city of Dunedin."[21]

Problems Continue

On June 3, 2012, a few months after RBC took control of the property, a St. Petersburg Times article reported that the historic Fenway was "blighted by graffiti." Broken glass, concrete, shingles, and other trash were scattered across the lawn.

Neighbors complained that children and vagrants were seen climbing through broken windows and rotting doors. Items were found in the hotel that indicated that someone was living there illegally.[22]

Another development was that Rahdert would be fined $250 a day, retroactive to June 2, for code violations. City officials said that these violations were a direct threat to public safety and were diminishing the property's value. A 23-page notice, listing these violations, was issued in January, 2012.[23]

National Register of Historic Places

Ironically, the state preliminarily approved that once renovation to the Fenway began, the hotel would be placed on the National Register of Historic Places [22]

The Future Looked Bleak

The future looked bleak for the Fenway Hotel as those who wanted the hotel saved watched helplessly, hoping for a happy ending.

St. Petersburg Times, June 3, 2012

St. Petersburg Times, June 3, 2012

THE FENWAY HOTEL

Chapter 11

Who Will Buy the Fenway?

2012-2014

L ike much of the history of the Fenway, this period had its drama and controversy. The bank began foreclosure proceedings on the property in February, 2010.

After foreclosure proceedings were filed, Rahdert presented at least one buyer to the bank, but the bank rejected the offer of $7.1 million.[1]

Rahdert decided that any decision made about the sale was now in the hands of the bank. The hotel remained empty and its future uncertain.[1]

Group Interested in the Fenway

Good news appeared on July 11, 2013 when the *Tampa Bay Times* reported that the Taoist Tai Chi Society of the United States of America was interested in purchasing the Fenway. The organization wanted to use the property as a practice space for people attending workshops and instruction, and a place for them to stay overnight.

There was already a Taoist Tai Chi Society headquarters in Toronto, Canada that had thousands of people a year visit from all over the world. The Fenway would become the

Society's headquarters in the United States. This area was selected because the late International Taoist Tai Chi Society founder, Master Moy Lin Sin, had visited the Tampa Bay area years before, and fell in love with it.[2]

Another Potential Buyer Emerged

In November 24, 2013, it was reported another potential buyer was interested in the hotel. James and Christy Bower, father and daughter developers from Pennsylvania, wanted to tear the hotel down and build an 88-room boutique hotel with the same name and look of the original Fenway. In order to do this, they needed permission from the City Commission.[3]

Mr. Bower had completed ten similar hotel projects in the Pennsylvania area. They believed taking down the Fenway structure and rebuilding was better than restoring it. Because of the condition of the building, they felt it would cost too much to fix, and rebuilding it would help guarantee the safety of guests.

A concrete and steel-reinforced building was planned with a courtyard, 27 to 33 waterside condos, and a 1920s interior, decorated with artifacts. There would be 11,000 to 19,000 square feet of conference space.[3]

The city expected to ask for the Local Planning Agency's support on December 19, 2013 and have a City Commission vote on January 9, 2014. With bank approval the couple wanted to close by January and start construction by February, 2014.[3]

The Bowers wanted a prompt decision because of a tight construction schedule that would allow the hotel to open for business by January, 2015.[3]

PNC Failed to Respond by Requested Date

The bank did not respond to the offer by 5:00 PM on November 27, 2013. The Bowers did not want to move forward without an agreement from the bank, so the buyers abandoned their plan of rebuilding the Fenway

The City Commission had drafted a development agreement to expedite the permitting process for the Bower's proposal. James Bower was disappointed that the sale did not go through and praised the city's readiness to work with him.

He stated how close they came to making the deal and blamed PNC bank for not responding to his offer in a timely manner.[4]

Bowers Reached Verbal Agreement

On March 8, 2014, it was confirmed that the Bowers from Pennsylvania had reached a verbal agreement with the PNC Bank to purchase the Fenway. James and Christy Bower received word that their offer was accepted – the purchase price was not revealed. The closing date was contingent on final approval by the city.

The plan was presented to neighbors, a citizen advisory board, and the City Commission. The property was in receivership so needed a judge's approval before they could purchase the property. If the city and bank approval was received by June, 2014, construction would start by September and open a year later.[5]

In April 23, 2014 the *Tampa Tribune* said that the "multimillion-dollar plan to raze the historic Fenway Hotel and rebuild it in the same architectural style is back on track after a delay in the property sale killed the property last year."[6]

On May 9, 2014, the *Tampa Bay Times* reported that City Commissioners gave their staff permission "to negotiate a development agreement" with the Bowers. The Local Planning Agency (citizen advisory board) discussed the agreement at a meeting held in May.[7]

Breakdown in Negotiations

In March, 2014, PNC had given the Bowers a verbal acceptance to their offer. Dunedin paved the way by approving many ordinance changes that would allow them to tear down and rebuild the hotel. The Bowers had spent a lot of money having architectural drawings done anticipating the final sale in July. 2014.[8]

It looked like the deal was done until an article in the *Tampa Bay Times* on May 30, 2014 reported that Christy Bowers said that PNC Bank had quit talking with her after a breakdown in negotiations.[8]

Residents and Merchants Made Their Voices Heard

Many residents and merchants preferred the property to be a public hotel and residential development. They demanded answers from the bank. The hotel would generate tax revenues if the hotel was sold to the Bowers. Since the Taoist Tai Chi Society is nonprofit, it would not pay taxes on the property.[8]

When residents found out that PNC had started talking with the Taoist Society, they began a protest by email, phone calls, and rallied a Facebook protest. The Downtown Dunedin Merchants Association mailed letters supporting the Bowers.[8]

Many residents thought Dunedin needed hotel space that the Fenway would provide.[9]

Taoist Tai Chi Society Bought the Property

A headline appeared on June 14, 2014: "Fenway Hotel Sold to Taoist Nonprofit."[10]   The national headquarters in Tallahassee was going to move to Dunedin. The Fenway would become an international conference center for the Taoist Tai Chi Society of the USA.

They planned to preserve and restore the hotel, not tear it down. Sean Dennison, Executive Director of the Taoist Tai Chi Society stated, "It's a jewel. It fits our needs and functions in an important way."[10]

An article in the *Tampa Tribune* stated, "The historical Fenway Hotel may again be a destination for visitors from across the nation and around the world, but not as a hotel."[11]

The purchase cost was reported to be $2.8 million. Dunedin would become an international gathering place for thousands of people from all over the world. No timeline for the restoration was given, but the plan was to renovate the guest rooms and common areas.

The hotel would open as a conference center, which would be open to the community. The group "was drawn to the ideal location and space provided at the old hotel but especially its unique aesthetics."[11]

Society Already Part of Dunedin Community

The Taoist Tai Chi Society had been part of the Dunedin community since 2004, when they began offering health-benefiting programs at the Hale Senior Activity Center at 330 Douglas Avenue. In 2010, after the membership had grown, the society moved to a new facility at 1370 Main Street.

Sean Dennison said, "As a dedicated member of the Dunedin community for years, we understand the historical importance of the Fenway and the warmth and love people have for this magnificent property."9

Society Paid off Lien on Property

On June 26, 2014, it was reported that the Taoist Tai Chi Society paid off nearly $109,000 in code enforcement liens. These had been accrued on the hotel property since 2012.

They did not challenge the liens and moved quickly to pay them off. Their next step was to have blueprints made and meet with city staff. [12]

Chapter 12

New Life for the Fenway

2014-

This chapter in the life of the Fenway started on a positive note. An article in the *Tampa Bay Times* reported plans for the hotel. Concerns of local residents were addressed and confirmed how much the Taoist Tai Chi Society wanted to be part of the community.

A series of meetings with neighbors and city advisory committees were held to secure approvals from city staff and commissioners. The Society needed to negotiate a development agreement to make sure the project met Dunedin's historical guidelines for the property.[1,2]

Plans for the Fenway

The Taoist Tai Chi Society planned to spend around $5 million to restore the Fenway. It would become a 102-room hotel for members from all over the world to stay there. Members of the Society would come for workshops, festivals, and conferences. The main building would include 3,000 square feet of meeting space, a 7,100 square foot atrium, a cafeteria, and 114 parking spots.[2]

The renovated Fenway would allow instruction and temporary lodging for its members. Conference space and meeting spaces would be available for community groups.[3]

An article published in the *Tampa Bay Times* (December 19, 2014) said that as many as 600 members at a time will attend events at the Fenway and the overflow of people will stay at local hotels.[4]

Fixing Up the Fenway

The building was believed to be in better shape than most people thought, especially those who wanted to tear it down. The steel frame and clay brick of the building showed no stress fractures.[2]

The Society hoped to get approval from city officials by the end of January, 2015, so they could begin renovating the hotel. Most of the restorations would be inside the hotel. The only exterior changes would be a new roof, new high impact glass windows, paint, and mold removal.[5]

Part of the Plan Changed

The original plan for the property after the Fenway was renovated was to replace the three buildings behind the hotel with twenty-seven two-story townhomes with two-car garages, a retention pond, a garden area and parking spaces. The Taoist Tai Chi Society wanted the townhomes to generate city and county tax revenue.

However, this changed in February, 2015, when neighbors objected to the townhouses, so the plan for building townhouses was eliminated. The Taoist Tai Chi Society decided to "drop its development ambitions and keep the good will of the community surrounding their property on Edgewater Drive."[6]

Renovation Continued

Taoist Tai Chi Society President Pegoty Packman said, "The project is not only of renovation, but of restoration, because construction plans have focused on transforming the structure's decrepit interior, while still striving to maintain the integrity of its exterior."[7]

Ownership Changed

While the Taoist Tai Chi Society was busy renovating the iconic Fenway, they continued hearing feedback that Dunedin residents were disappointed that the hotel would not be available to the public.

In May 2016, a newspaper article told about an agreement with the Tampa-based hotel developer, Mainsail Lodging & Development. They would take over the renovation and manage the hotel.[8]

Wanting to be an integral part of the community, the nonprofit charitable organization decided to partner with Mainsail Lodging & Development. This would make the hotel available to the public, except when Taoist Tai Chi Society members came into town for conferences and instruction.[8]

The City of Dunedin Commissioners approved an amendment to a development agreement on June 15, 2017 for Mainsail to acquire the western acres of the property, while the Taoist Tai Chi Society maintained ownership of the eastern 1.838 acres.[9]

On December 2017, the Taoist Tai Chi Society transferred 3.358 acres of the Fenway Hotel property to the Mainsail Fenway Hotel LLLP.

The New Fenway Hotel

The newly renovated Fenway Hotel is a one-of-a-kind boutique hotel, with 83 guest rooms and suites. Unique to the hotel is the Hi-Fi Rooftop Bar, a resort-style pool, a signature restaurant called the HEW Parlor & Chophouse with an open kitchen featuring counter service, intimate banquettes and private dining options.[10]

The hotel consists of 10,000 square feet of event space, a ballroom, and areas with live entertainment that will bring back memories of the hotel's musical past.[10]

Mainsail Lodging & Development's founder and president, Joe Collier said, "We are going to tap into all things offered in Dunedin – the Blue Jays, Caladesi and Honeymoon Islands, the great downtown food scene, the Pinellas Trail, the waterfront. We have a lot to work with here."[10]

He continued, "The unique history of the Fenway Hotel and the community of Dunedin inspired our vision for the property. The new Fenway will bring together touches of the past in a modern setting, giving new life to the hotel and restoring a piece of the destination's charming, offbeat character."[10]

National Register of Historic Places

The new owners began immediately to work to nominate the Fenway to be listed on the National Register of Historic Places. The nomination went before the State Review Committee in August, 2018.

The building could be listed as soon as January, 2019 and will join four other historical places in Dunedin that have this distinction: (1) J. O. Douglas House, (2)

Andrews Memorial Chapel, (3) Blatchley House, and the (4) Dunedin Isles Golf Club.

The National Register of Historic Places is the "official list of the Nation's historic places worthy of preservation. National Register properties have significance to the history of their community state, or the nation."[11]

We Have Our Happy Ending

The Fenway Hotel has done it again! Over the years some people thought the hotel was too far gone to save. Some said to consider the Fenway site for nothing but a park. The hotel was called a "white elephant" and a "dinosaur," but they were wrong.

Others saw the beauty and history of the Fenway, located in a very delightful town, and wanted the hotel to survive.

The Fenway Hotel has enjoyed a long and colorful history. Despite many challenges and setbacks, the hotel continues to survive and adds to the history and charm of Dunedin.

Those who have loved the Fenway Hotel over the years are grateful that it has been saved. Guests from all over the world will enjoy a unique hotel experience along with appreciating the best that Dunedin and the Tampa Bay area has to offer!

HOTEL FENWAY

Color Photos

"The Fenway"
Hand-Colored Postcard

"The Fenway on Clearwater Bay"
1938 Postcard

"Recreation Lounge in the Fenway"
Postcard

"Main Lounge in the Fenway"
Postcard

Aerial View of Fenway, 1974 "Harvester"

Taoist Tai Chi Society, Photographer: Frank Duffy

Artist's Rendition of the Fenway Hotel – 2018
Permission of Mainsail Lodging & Development

Artist's Rendition of the Hi-Fi Rooftop Bar - 2018
Permission of Mainsail Lodging & Development

References

Chapter 1: A New Hotel in Dunedin

[1] The proposed Fenway Hotel for Dunedin: help the project along. *Dunedin Times*. July 3, 1924, p 1.

[2] Projects go over the top. *Dunedin Times*, July 10, 1924, p 1.

[3] $300,000 hotel now started: workmen on ground. *Dunedin Times*. September 11, 1924, p 1.

[4] Author unknown. The Fenway Hotel architecture. n.d.

[5] Hotel designer's rites tomorrow. *The Evening Independent*. February 25, 1937, p 2.

[6] Fenway Hotel owners changed, *Clearwater Sun*, July 31, 1925, p 1.

[7] Radio outfit has arrived at Dunedin: largest station in south. *Dunedin Times*. August 13, 1925, p 1.

[8] Davidson, William L. Dunedin…Through the Years 1850-1978. Charlotte, NC: Delmar Printing Co.1978, 1988 p 75-6.

[9] Radio at Fenway: ready Jan'y 1. *Dunedin Times*. September 3, 1925, p 1.

[10] Dedication of WGHB station on Saturday night. *Dunedin Times*. December 3, 1925, p 1.

[11] Grace Clark, 87, pioneer of Pinellas County Radio (obituary), *St. Petersburg Times*, January 15, 1991, p 7.

[12] Organ recitals will be put on air at station. *St. Petersburg Times*. April 26, 1926, p 12, sec 2.

[13] First daylight radio program given by WGHB. *St. Petersburg Times*. January 10, 1927.

[14] Expect Fenway Hotel to be ready for occupancy by mid-December. *The Evening Independent*. October 2, 1926, p 3.

[15] Order assures completion of Dunedin Hotel. *St. Petersburg Times*. October 3, 1926, p 7.

[16] Radio station's name unchanged. *The Evening Independent*, July 5, 1926, p 3A.

[17] Radio aerials will be moved to city park. *The Evening Independent*. November 3, 1926, p 3A.

[18] Miskind, Barry. Radio History by the Bay. *Radio Guide*, May 2003, p. 4.

[19] Start work on completion of Fenway Hotel. *Dunedin Times*. October 14, 1926, p 1.

Chapter 2: James H. Batachelder Leases the Hotel

[1] Fenway Hotel will open January 5th. *Dunedin Times*. December 23,mm 1926. P 1.

[2] Fenway Hotel in Dunedin leased for three years. *The Evening Independent*. December 30, 1926, p 3A.

[3] Dinner Dance reservations are over 200. *Dunedin Times*. January 6, 1927, p 1.

[4] Fenway Hotel at Dunedin is sold. *The Evening Independent*. August 9, 1928, p 6.

[5] Fenway Hotel on sale today. *The Evening Independent*. October 1, 1928, p 8.

[6] City to foreclose on Hotel Fenway property soon. *Dunedin Times*. January 17, 1929, p 1.

[7] J.H. Batchelder leases Hotel Dunedin. *Dunedin Times*. January 10, 1929, p 1.

[8] Big hotel opens at Dunedin next year. *St. Petersburg Times*, March 24, 1929.

[9] James H. McGill buys the Fenway. *Evening Independent*. July 20, 1929. P 4A.

[10] Fenway Hotel purchased by Indiana man. *Dunedin Times*. July 18, 1929, p 1.

Chapter 3: James McGill Buys the Fenway; It Becomes a Fabulous Hotel

[1] Grant, Vivien S. Fenway-On-The-Gulf. Based on a talk at Schiller International University. 1997.

[2] Fenway Hotel purchased by Indiana man. *Dunedin Times*. July 18, 1929, p 1.

[3] Hotel Fenway sold; reopens this winter. *Clearwater Sun*. July 19, 1929, p 1-2.

[4] Fenway hostelry being remodeled. *The Evening Independent*. August 22, 1929, p 4.

[5] Fenway Hotel opens season. *Clearwater Sun*. December 27, 1929, p 1.

[6] Hotel Fenway is filling up. *St. Petersburg Times*. January 6, 1930, p 3.

[7] Fenway closes successful season April 1. *Dunedin Times*. April 4, 1930, p 1.

[8] Fenway-on-the-Gulf guests enjoy social activities, *St. Petersburg Times*, February 27, 1938, Section 2.

[9] C. Darrow is guest at Fenway. *Dunedin Times*. February 20, 1931, p 1.

[10] Dunedin News Notes. *St. Petersburg Times*. March 10, 1931, p 10.

[11] LaFollette at Fenway on opening. *Dunedin Times*. January 5, 1933, p.1

[12] Carbide Company official visits at Hotel Fenway. *The Evening Independent*, February 12, 1934.

[13] Guests of note registered at Hotel Fenway. *Dunedin Times*. January 25, 1935, p 1.

[14] Fenway guests to linger late. *St. Petersburg Times*. April 1, 1937, p 9.

[15] Famous explorer heard by guests of Hotel Fenway. *The Evening Independent*. March 21, 1940.

[16] Secretary to President Roosevelt spends two weeks here at Fenway. *Dunedin Times*. March 5, 1943, p 1.

[17] Blackstone, Lillian. Secretary to F.D.R. ends two-week visit to Dunedin. *St. Petersburg Times*. February 27, 1943, p 1,11.

[18] Fenway, Dunedin Hotels to reopen. *The Evening Independent*. November 4, 1943, p 4.

[19] Fenway building swimming beach along bay shore. *The Evening Independent*. November 2, 1934, p 3.

[20] Hotel Fenway opens Saturday for 7th season. *Dunedin Times*, December 19, 1935.

[21] Hotel Fenway opens at Dunedin Dec. 19. *St. Petersburg Times*. December 16, 1936, p 22.

[22] Channel, dock improvements at Fenway started. *The Evening Independent*. June 20, 1938, p 7.

[23] Hotel Fenway to Open for 10th Season. *Dunedin Times*, December 16, 1938, p 1.

[24] Hotel Fenway opens season December 28. *Dunedin Times.* December 27, 1940, p 1.

[25] Fenway guests become Dunedin home owners. *Dunedin Times.* January 24, 1941, p 1.

[26] Expect good season. *Dunedin Times.* January 2, 1942, p 1.

[27] Fenway Hotel ends season. *St. Petersburg Times.* April 13, 1945, p 17.

Chapter 4: C.T. Scanlan Buys the Fenway

[1] C.T. Scanlan buys Fenway Hotel. *St. Petersburg Times.* August 5, 1945, p 4.

[2] C.T. Scanlan purchases the Fenway. *Dunedin Times.* August 10, 1945, p 1.

[3] Fenway closes 22nd successful season Tuesday. *Dunedin Times.* April 6, 1951, p 1.

[4] Mrs. C.T. Scanlan passes away Wed.; services held Sat. *Dunedin Times* November 13, 1953, p 1.

[5] Grant, Vivien S. Fenway-On-The-Gulf. Based on a talk at Schiller International University. 1997.

[6] Fenway sold yesterday. *Dunedin Times.* August 23, 1956, p 1.

[7] Sutton, Kathy. Fenway: it was fabulous. *Clearwater Sun,* May 15, 1983. p 1C-2C.

[8] Cosdon, Christina K. Charles Scanlan, business leader. *St. Petersburg Times.* October 19, 1990, p 13.

Chapter 5: Marius Pauchey Opens the Fenway Year-Round

[1] Fenway sold yesterday. *Dunedin Times*. August 23, 1956, p 1.

[2] Hill, Norma Jean. Dunedin's Fenway hotel sold. *St. Petersburg Times*. August 23, 1956, p 27.

[3] Midwest operator buys Clearwater Beach Hotel. *St. Petersburg Times*. August 25, 1955, p 23.

[4] Dunedin's Fenway Hotel starts 1957 season Saturday under new owner. *St. Petersburg Times*. December 27, 1956, p 23.

[5] The Fenway will open Saturday. *Dunedin Times*. December 27, 1956, p 1.

[6] Fenway Pool will be open to public Monday, June 3. *Dunedin Times*. May 23, 1957, p 1.

[7] Fenway Pool will open on June 4 for second season. *Dunedin Times*, May 29, 1958, p 1.

[8] Hotel Fenway 31st Season opens Friday. *St. Petersburg Times*. December 31, 1957, p 3-B.

[9] Grant, Vivien S. Fenway-On-The-Gulf. Based on a talk at Schiller International University. 1997.

[10] Fenway Hotel leased by Blair Enterprises. *St. Petersburg Times*. November 12, 1959. p 13-B.

Chapter 6: Richard Blair Introduces "Lifetime Residency Program"

[1] Fenway Hotel leased by Blair Enterprises. *St. Petersburg Times*. November 12, 1959, p 13-B.

[2] The Fenway leased by Richard Blair; will open for season on January 2. *Dunedin Times*. November 12, 1959, p 1.

[3] Dunedin Hotel to operate on all-year basis. *The Evening Independent.* December 21, 1959. p 1.

[4] Hotel Fenway to open Saturday. *St. Petersburg Times*, December 31, 1959.

[5] Fenway Hotel is purchased by Blair Inc. *St. Petersburg Times,* July 7, 1960, p 1-B.

[6] Blair Enterprises buys the Fenway Hotel and property on Edgewater. *Dunedin Times.* July 7, 1960, p 1.

7 The Fenway Hotel will feature new retirement plan. *Dunedin Times.* September 8, 1960, p 1.

[8] Lanpher, Dr. Bill W. He is Able: Trinity College of Florida's Foundations and Early Years. Xulon Press, 2005.

[9] Fenway hotel changes hands, will be academy. *St. Petersburg Times.* June 30, 1961, p 15-B.

[10] Duncan Hines Institute, Inc. Duncan Hines Vacation Guide, Ithaca, NY: Duncan Hines Institute. 1961. p. 115.

Chapter 7: Trinity College Turns the Fenway into a Campus

[1] Lanpher, Dr. Bill W. He is Able: Trinity College of Florida's Foundations and Early Years. Xulon Press, 2005.

[2] Gathering in praise of their enduring mission. *The St. Petersburg Times.* May 8, 2007, p 1 (Largo Times).

[3] Lucas, Brock. Billy Graham's college comes of age. *St. Petersburg Times.* August 21, 1965, p 1,3.

[4] Pugh, Jeanne. Billy Graham: from Florida Bible Institute to the World's ...pulpit. *St. Petersburg Times.* March 17, 1979, p 1,3.

[5] Billy Graham: he received his calling in the Bay area. *Evening Independent.* October 3, 1964, p 7-A.

[6] New college to open here. *St. Petersburg Times.* May 6, 1946, p 613.

[7] Davis, Paul A. Bible College buys famed night spot. *The Evening Independent.* January 16, 1951, p 6.

[8] Fenway hotel changes hands, will be academy. *St. Petersburg Times.* June 30, 1961, 15-B.

[9] Fenway is prep school. *St. Petersburg Times.* August 3, 1963, p 3-D.

[10] Billy Graham due at college. *St. Petersburg Times.* January 21, 1965.

[11] 60 graduated at Trinity. *St. Petersburg Times.* May 16, 1966, p 1-B, 7-B.

[12] Trinity planning open house. *St. Petersburg Times.* September 24, 1969, p 5-B.

[13] College land may go for new apartments. *St. Petersburg Times.* August 9, 1969, p 7-B.

[14] Belleair okays U.S. Steel rezoning plan. *St. Petersburg Times.* April 2, 1970.

[15] Well done thou good and faithful servant. Trinity Yearbook. Genesis 1982, p 99.

[16] Youmans, Marty. Trinity College on verge of leaving Dunedin. *Suncoast News.* May 22, 1985.

[17] Squitieri, Al. A Dunedin institution may be moving to Tarpon Spring. *Dunedin Times.* May 31, 1985, p 1.

[18] Trinity College closes out three decades in Dunedin. *Dunedin Times.* June 6, 1988, p 1.

[19] Windom, Ebony. Little college that could and will. *St. Petersburg Times*, July 31, 2004, p 4.

[20] Youmans, Marty. Trinity sets to relocate. *Clearwater Sun*, August, 26, 1985.

Chapter 8: What to Do with the Fenway?
[1] Mauer, Elizabeth. Dunedin may buy Trinity College. *St. Petersburg Times*. March 5, 1985, p 1,5.

[2] Smith, Michael. Report finds college not feasible as city hall. *The Suncoast News*, November 30, 1985, p 1.

[3] Mauer, Elizabeth. Dunedin commissioners end plans to buy Trinity College. *St. Petersburg Times*. November 30, 1985, p 1.

[4] Staff Writer. Developer applies to Dunedin for rezoning of Trinity property. *St. Petersburg Times*. December 10, 1985, p 3.

[5] Mauer, Elizabeth. Dunedin votes against condos. *St. Petersburg Times*, January 24, 1986, p 1,14.

[6] Steinle, Diane. Dunedin tries to interest Blue Jays in buying college. *St. Petersburg Times*. January 8, 1987, p 3.

[7] Steinle, Diane. Blue Jays won't buy building – Team does not have money for Trinity property in Dunedin. *St. Petersburg Times*. March 19, 1987, p 3.

[8] Subko, Kathy. Trinity College might be retirement center. *St. Petersburg Times*. November 18, 1987, p 1,6.

[9] Cosdon, Christina K. Residents' views vary on retirement center proposal. *St. Petersburg Times*. November 20, 1987, p 8.

[10] Subko, Kathy. Trinity College sells waterfront property. *St. Petersburg Times*. April 28, 1988, p 1,6.

[11] Subko, Kathy. College president praises buyers of Dunedin property. *St. Petersburg Times*. April 29, 1988, p 3.

[12] Tuck, Angela Duerson. Owners to seek historic status for former Trinity College campus. *St. Petersburg Times*. Jun 11, 1988, p 3.

[13] Tuck, Angela Duerson. Ex-Trinity College site is up for sale. *St. Petersburg Times*. October 1, 1988, p 1.

[14] Tuck, Angela Duerson. Trinity building plan denied in Dunedin. *St. Petersburg Times*. October 14,1988, p 6.

[15] Tuck, Angela Duerson. Dunedin rejects transformation of Trinity. *St. Petersburg Times*. November 18, 1988, p 1.

[16] Tuck, Angela Duerson. New use sought for college property. *St. Petersburg Times*. November 22, 1988, p 3.

[17] Tuck, Angela Duerson. Hotel plans considered for mansion. *St. Petersburg Times*. December 17, 1988, p 7.

[18] Tuck, Angela Duerson. Developer pulls out of Trinity study. *St. Petersburg Times*. February 3, 1989, p 1.

[19] Tuck, Angela Duerson. Dunedin property sale unlikely: Owners want to sell a portion of former Trinity College site. *St. Petersburg Times*. February 16, 1989, p 1.

[20] Caldwell, Alicia. Dunedin landmark near sale. *St. Petersburg Times*. September 28, 1989, p 6.

[21] Jones, Patrice. Buyers of Trinity College site file suit. *St. Petersburg Times*. December 6, 1989, p 1,8.

[22] Griffin, Laura. Architect sues Trinity to collect bills for work. *St. Petersburg Times*. December 14, 1989, p 6.

[23] Jones, Patrice. Architect sues over Trinity site: Property owner faces a $15,000 claim. *St. Petersburg Times*. December 16, 1989, p 3.

[24] Lednicer, Lisa Grace. Couple sues Dunedin over zoning change. *St. Petersburg Times.* November 1, 1990, p 3.

Chapter 9: Schiller International University's First Campus in the United States

[1] Jones, Patrice. Educator buys Trinity college land. *St. Petersburg Times.* March 4, 1990, p 1.

[2] Leibrecht, Christoph. Schiller International University: Thirty years of International Education, n.d.

[3] The Internationalization of Schiller University: preparing students for a global economy. Compass: The Association of Independent Colleges and Schools. 52:10. November 1989.

[4] Jones, Patrice. International glance given to Trinity site. *St. Petersburg Times*, January 24, 1990, p 3.

[5] Mucci, Paul. Zoning exception clears way for sale of Trinity College site. *Suncoast News*, March 3, 1990.

[6] We have our own university. *Dunedin Times*, March 8, 1990, p 1.

[7] Jones, Patrice, University gets okay to build at Trinity site. St. Petersburg Times, March 1, 1990

[8] Jones, Patrice. Trinity buildings primp for the university life. *St. Petersburg Times.* July 17, 1990,

[9] Pilugin, Nicholas W. Decayed landmark becomes a college. *Tampa Tribune*, December 2, 1990, p 1.

[10] Lednicer, Lisa Grace. College prepares a classy campus. *St. Petersburg Times*, December 17, 1990, p 1.

[11] Kirkham, Bruce. University ends first semester. *Tampa Tribune*, May 3, 1991 p 1.

[12] Various minutes, invitations, and programs from the Schiller Friends of the Library.

[13] Lieb, Patricia. Local university open to new students. *Suncoast News*, August 14, 1993.

[14] Riley, Jim. University moving offices to Dunedin. *The Tampa Tribune*. August 12, 1994, p 1.

[15] Davis, Karin. Program makes a world of a difference – a university program teaches students about world issues and the United Nations. *The Tampa Tribune*. April 26, 1996, p1.

[16] Tribune Staff Report. Schiller students to stage United Nations session. *The Tampa Tribune*. March 22, 1995, p 3.

[17] Schantz, Mark. International flavor: Public is invited as Schiller University students cook up a unique dining experience at twice monthly dinners. *The Suncoast News*. February 4, 2004.

[18] Collins, Lesley. Schiller to expand high school. *The Tampa Tribune*. June 20, 1998, p 6.

[19] Hirsch, Deborah. Sept. 11 stems flow of foreign students. *St. Petersburg Times*. May 19, 2002, p 7.

[20] Raman, Sheela. Dunedin approves hotel revival. *St. Petersburg Times*. November 18, 2006.

[21] Helfand, Lorri. Schiller hopeful for a Largo opening in August. *St. Petersburg Times*. July 5, 2006, p 1.

[22] Beal, Nova. Schiller University founder is dead at 79. *St. Petersburg Times*, March 1, 2007, p 7-B.

Chapter 10: George Rahdert Plans to Restore the Fenway

[1] Reeves, Terri Bryce. More Fenway glory days ahead? - An attorney's restoration plan is welcomed as good news for Dunedin. *St. Petersburg Times*. November 6, 2005, p 1-B.

[2] El-Khoury, Tamara. Schiller site may become hotel, condos. *St. Petersburg Times*. November 4, 2005, p 1-B.

[3] Raman, Sheela. Dunedin approves hotel revival. *St. Petersburg Times*. November 18, 2006, p 1.

[4] Battle over historic hotel requires common ground. Times Editorial. *St. Petersburg Times*. April 20, 2006,

[5] De La Torre, Vanessa. Neighbors prepared to fight hotel plans for "years." *St. Petersburg Times*. April 16, 2006, p 1-B.

[6] Graham, T. James. Hotel Fenway plan as asset. *St. Petersburg Times*. April 30, 2006, p 2-B.

[7] Jones, Sandra. Restored hotel will be great asset. *St. Petersburg Times*. November 13, 2006, p 2-B.

[8] Tilly, Mark A. Neighborhood's future will be at stake. *St. Petersburg Times*. November 13, 2006, p 2B.

[9] Clark, Ashlee. Plans to change Schiller rejected. *St. Petersburg Times*. June 17, 2006, p 1-B.

[10] Raman, Sheela. Developer hopes Dunedin smiles on scaled-back hotel. *St. Petersburg Times*. November 7, 2006, p 1-B.

[11] Potential for hotel is better than eyesore. *St. Petersburg Times*. November 26, 2006, p 2-B.

[12] El-Khoury, Tamara. Developer scales back project. *St. Petersburg Times*. May 17, 2007, p 2-B.

[13] Steinle, Diane. Fenway Hotel benefits from common ground. *St Petersburg Times*. May 27, 2007, p 2-B. 15

[14] Caldwell, Alexandra. Fenway Hotel may get new lease on life. *Dunedin Beacon.* March 26, 2009, p 1

[15] Fenway by the bay is moving closer to glory. *Tampa Bay Times*. April 5, 2009.

[16] Commission approves new hotel agreement. *St. Petersburg Times*. March 28, 2009, p 3-B.

[17] Cashill, Margaret. Dunedin hotel site on track for preservation. *Tampa Bay Business Journal.* June 17, 2009,

[18] Harwell, Drew. Developer gets approval to renovate Dunedin's Fenway Hotel. *Tampa Bay Times*. August 21, 2009.

[19] Harwell, Drew. Developer needs cash to finish Fenway resort renovation in Dunedin. *St. Petersburg Times*. December 20, 2009, p 1-B.

[20] Harwell, Drew. Developer for Fenway hotel in Dunedin hit with foreclosure lawsuit. *St. Petersburg Times* February 10, 2010, p 1-B.

[21] Summers, Keyonna. Historic Fenway Hotel will be auctioned Wednesday. *Tampa Bay Times*. March 29, 2012, p 1-B.

[22] Summers, Keyonna. Squalor may come to an end. *Tampa Bay Times*. June 3, 2012, p 1.

[23] Summers, Keyonna. Fenway Hotel owner faces fine of $250 a day for code violations. *St. Petersburg Times*. June 7, 2012,

Chapter 11: Who Will Buy the Fenway?

[1] Summers, Keyonna. Bank merger delays auction of Dunedin's Fenway Hotel. *Tampa Bay Times*. April 5, 2012.

[2] Summers, Keyonna Tai chi organization wants to buy Fenway Hotel. *Tampa Bay Times*, July 11, 2013, p 3-B.

[3] Summers, Keyonna. Fenway purchase close. *Tampa Bay Times*, November 24, 2013, p 1,11.

[4] Summers, Keyonna. Fenway Hotel acquisition falls through. *Tampa Bay Times*, December 4, 2013, p1, 12.

[5] Summers, Keyonna, Pair to buy iconic Dunedin Hotel, *Tampa Bay Times*, March 8, 2014, p 3-B.

[6] Boatwright, Josh. Dunedin's Fenway Hotel redux renewed – plan to raze it, build modernized version is back. *The Tampa Tribune*, April 23, 2014, p 4.

[7] Preliminary approval for two projects, *Tampa Bay Times*, May 9, 2014, p 3.

[8] Summers, Keyonna. Fenway Hotel deal looks to be in jeopardy. *Tampa Bay Times*. May 30, 2014, p 8-B.

[9] Schantz, Mark. Taoist Tai Society completes purchase of Fenway Hotel. *The Tampa Tribune*. June 19, 2014, p 3.

[10] Frago, Charlie. Fenway Hotel sold to Taoist Nonprofit. *Tampa Bay Times*, June 14, 2014, p 3-B.

[11] Boatwright, Josh. Fenway Hotel in Dunedin sold – historical property's buyer, Taoist Tai Chi Society, won't raze it. *The Tampa Tribune*, June 14, 2014, p 1.

[12] New owner pays Fenway Hotel liens, *Tampa Bay Times*, June 26, 2014, p 1.

Chapter 12: New Life for the Fenway

[1] Summers, Keyonna. Fenway Hotel owners outline vision. *Tampa Bay Times*. September 4, 2014.

[2] Summers, Keyonna. Fenway owners pressed. *Tampa Bay Times*. November 21, 2014, p 1.

[3] Schantz, Mark. Dunedin officials hear initial plans for $14 million Fenway Hotel renovation. *Clearwater Gazette*. September 25, 2014.

[4] Summers, Keyonna. Fenway plan clears hurdles. *Tampa Bay Times*. December 19, 2014. P 1, 4.

[5] Boatwright, Josh. Tai Chi to renovate Fenway Hotel. *Tampa Bay Times,* December 23, 2014.

[6] Boatwright, Josh. Fenway rehab gets OK after town homes plans dropped. *Tampa Tribune*, February 25, 2015.

[7] Reeves, Megan. Fenway renovations done with great care. *Tampa Bay Times*, March 18, 2016.

[8] Reeves, Megan. A partnership will turn the historic Fenway into a public boutique hotel: Dunedin gets its wish. *Tampa Bay Times*. May 18, 2016.

[9] Germond, Tom. City Oks changes to Fenway development plans. *TBNWeekly.com*. June 28, 2017.

[10] Harrell, Donovan. Historic Fenway in Dunedin set to reopen as boutique hotel in September. *Tampa Bay Times*. March 23, 2018.

[11] National Register of Historic Places Program. https://www.nps.gov/nr/faq.htm#nr. Accessed July 6, 2018.